A TRUE CONNECTION – CHRISTIAN DEVOTIONAL FOR TEEN GIRLS

DEEPEN YOUR RELATIONSHIP WITH GOD AND START TO FULLY EMBRACE YOURSELF WITH THESE 5-MINUTE DEVOTIONS + LIFE-CHANGING SPIRITUAL EXERCISES

HILLARY OLIVE

I dedicate this book to my mom, my grandma, and my mother-in-law.
No words can describe how grateful I am for these women.

CONTENTS

SPECIAL GIFT
JUST FOR YOU!

THIS BUNDLE INCLUDES:
A 'CONNECT WITH CHRIST' WORKSHEET TO HELP YOU
DETERMINE WHAT IS HOLDING YOU BACK FROM HAVING THE
CONNECTION YOU NEED

'FEELING SOME TYPE OF WAY' LIST OF 15 SCRIPTURES YOU
CAN JUMP TO AT ANY TIME WHEN LIFE GETS HARD

'HOST, LEAD, AND SUCCEED' YOUR STEP-BY-STEP GUIDE TO
CREATING A BRAND NEW BIBLE STUDY GROUP

INTRODUCTION

Hi, I'm Olivia—a former teenager who struggled to know who God is, who battled to believe God was genuinely and personally interested in me. It caused unnecessary angst during my teenage years, trying to figure it all out.

But I did. I was in my mid-twenties when it happened, so if you aren't 'there' yet, don't give up. Trust me when I say you can do this.

The more accurate way to explain my relationship with God would be to say that I was in my mid-twenties when I finally started to understand God's steadfast love for me and what it means to have a personal relationship with Him. You see, just like many of you, I spent my teens and early twenties wanting desperately to fit in with my peers. I wanted to look, think, and act like everyone else. I wanted to be cool. I just didn't always know-how. Everyone else made it look so easy, yet things changed every time I got close to getting it right. Styles…food fads…music, sports, and movie icons…slang… even the 'right' phone changed too often for me to keep up. Instead, all these changes left me feeling even more confused and trying extra hard but not getting anywhere—anywhere in the right direction, that is.

I didn't understand at the time that everyone I was trying to keep up with was probably just as lost and confused as I was. Everyone was trying to make their way in the world to pursue happiness and fulfillment. Like a lot of you, I was a child of divorced parents. I was three when they divorced. My parents were at opposite ends of the spectrum regarding religion and spirituality. My dad and his family were non-practicing Catholics. My mom and her family are Jewish. On top of that, my dad passed away when I was fifteen.

The only similarity between Mom and Dad regarding their spirituality was that neither one was too concerned about pursuing God on a personal level or teaching me how to. Like most couples in that position, they decided to expose my siblings and me to both sides so that we would be cultur-ally aware and decide for ourselves when we were older how or if we wanted to pursue God.

My grandparents (my mom's parents) are lovely and incred-ibly kind people who are super-devoted to their Jewish faith. I spent a significant amount of time with them, *and* I loved every minute I spent with them, which means they had more influence on my views of God and religion. I attended a Jewish Sunday school and summer camp. I went to the temple on Fridays with them to celebrate Shabbat and enjoyed cooking the traditional foods for the holidays. I felt like I knew all *about* God.

And then came college....

If you are a college student, you know exactly what I'm talking about. If you are not a college student yet, you will. Anyway, let me just say that going to college is incredible. It's amazing! But it is also challenging. You are caught in that time warp of being a kid who is expected to make adult choices and decisions, while at the same time, you are encouraged to live it up because your days of being able to do that are numbered. When you do not have a personal relationship with God before you go off to college, the busyness of it all could send your spirituality to the wayside. That's pretty much what happened to me.

I did not consider myself a practicing Jewish girl by my first year of college. I went home for holidays for the love of traditions and family gatherings, but the connection to the faith was lost to me. I adopted a term coined by millennials as "spiritual, not religious," which worked for a while until it didn't. I looked for God in yoga, meditation, and self-help books. Those all helped me become a well-rounded person, but eventually, I felt spiritually dried up. I always prayed, but my prayers became stale. I was praying out of habit, not out of love. Then, I met Jesus. When I walked into my new church home, something hit me like a train to the heart. Tears rolled down my face. I knew I was in the right place. I knew I did not have to search anymore. I accepted Jesus as my Lord and Savior and soon after was Baptized. I felt so-called to write this book. Saying Yes to Jesus completely transformed my life and my family's life. No, my grandparents were not upset. When I told them I was a Christian, it was met with love, kindness, and genuine happiness because I found what I didn't even know I was looking for.

The life of a teen girl is hard. You are trying to live your best life each day, sprinkled with the need to make solid adult decisions while school demands, extracurriculars, and friends compete to be at the forefront of your focus. It's exhausting! With all this constant doing and all these things competing for your time and energy, where is God in all this? He's right there alongside you, but when do you show up for Him? A couple of hours on Sunday? God is the reason for all the things we get to do and all the people we get to see, and yet Pew Research conducted a study in 2014 that found that only an average of 55% of Americans pray daily.

Let's get those numbers higher and make a change together. God is in everything and wants to be a part of your everyday life so let's give Him daily praise and gratitude for everything (Ephesians 5:20). Whether you are in high school, college, or even just out of college—the one thing you can know for sure is this: Y'all **need Jesus. *We* all need Jesus.**

He is the only one who can make sense of anything and everything. He is the only real hope there is. He is the only 'thing' that will never let us down. Even when we do not put God first, He is still first. God is the real deal. The complete package. He never gives up on us. He never lies, cheats, or tricks us. God does not misuse and abuse. He does not do anything that is not best for us...not just good, but best for us. The only things that God asks and expects in return for doing all of that are faith and trust. He wants us to have complete faith and trust in Him instead of just trying to squeak by life or fake a relationship with him.

Now for the best part of all—Jesus doesn't expect or even want you to attempt this level of faith and obedience on your own. He doesn't expect it because he knows it isn't possible. And the last thing he wants you to do is to fail, which is why he said in Matthew 28:20b, "And surely I am with you always, to the very end of the age."

My friend Faith said recently, "Getting to know God takes a whole lot of love and a little discipline." This book will discuss the necessary discipline we need to constantly and forever continue to deepen and grow our relationship with God. You'll learn so many ways to reach out to God that it'll all be second nature before long. Jesus will be so rooted into every fiber of your being that your light will shine so bright that people will feel it and be blessed by it.

Wanting. Believing. Seeking.

You need these three steps to have a genuine connection with God. All you must do is want it. It's that simple. All you have to do is say, "God, I want to know you more," and He will light the way on which steps to take. If you genuinely believe that, you've already accomplished steps 1 and 2. It's that simple; you have already committed to the first two steps. Just by you being here, you are actively seeking God's face. Seeking is the discipline part. In this book, you will find suggested exercises to help deepen your relationship with God and fully embrace the intelligent, compassionate, and impactful girl you are. *A True Connection* is designed to meet you where you are, whether you are a new believer or have been in Sunday school your whole life.

Now that I've told you quite a bit about myself (hopefully it wasn't TMI), I am going to tell you why I wrote this book:

- I've been where you are now.
- I do not want anyone to go through the confusion I went through.
- There are many unique ways to develop your relationship with God through Christ Jesus, and I want to help you find your way.
- Because you matter, and you deserve it.

This book is NOT a replacement for the Bible. No book is. The Bible is the ultimate guidebook for living life no matter the situation or circumstance. This book is a tool to use with your Bible. Each short devotion consists of an accurate and relevant story to make you think, help you realize you are not alone and give you the push of encouragement you need to make Jesus the Lord and Savior of your life. To make him real and personal to YOU.

Are you ready to do that? Or, at the very least, are you prepared to investigate the possibility? Are you ready to get to know Jesus for who he is and open yourself up to him? I pray wholeheartedly that you are willing to try because if you do, Jesus will be there to meet you and help you take just one baby step at a time until you are totally committed to being whom He created you to be.

Jesus, I pray that everyone who reads this book will give you a chance to be their Lord and Savior. I pray that they will learn to believe in you and trust you wholeheartedly. I pray they will get to know you personally and feel you with every fiber of their being. I pray that the Holy Spirit comes into their soul and ignites their spirit on fire for you, Lord. May their light shine so bright that everyone who encounters them will be blessed by it. May no girl ever feel alone because you are with them. God, no matter what, you are always there. May every girl know how to call upon you for every situation, season, and day of their life Lord. I pray that every single girl knows they are truly loved, magnificent, and unique in every way. I pray that every girl knows that you are the best and only solution for life because you are the giver of life. Amen.

1

ONLY THE REAL THING WILL DO

Do not merely listen to the word and so deceive yourselves. Do what it says. Anyone who listens to the word but does not do what it says is like someone who looks at his face in a mirror and, after looking at himself, goes away and immediately forgets what he looks like.

— *JAMES 1:22-24 NIV*

Were you ever that kid who bit into the fake fruit on your grandma's table, only to find out it wasn't real? Or have you ever been disappointed or surprised that the actors of a movie or TV show didn't like each other (that's putting it mildly) in real life, even though they were best friends when the cameras were rolling?

Fake fruit phony relationships look pretty, make our mouths water, could make us smile, laugh, and 'lose' ourselves for a while, and even convince us that something is real even when it is not. These deceptions only work for a little bit, however. Sooner or later, the truth comes out. It never fails. Why? Because lies—no matter how big, small, innocent, or deliberate—always trip themselves up.

Not so with God and Jesus. God's opinion on EVERY-THING is truth. He can't lie. And since Jesus is God's Son, the personification of God himself (more on that later), it is equally impossible for him to lie.

Don't let those facts intimidate you. No, seriously, don't. Use them for your good. Recognize Jesus for who and what he is —the only one who can help you navigate life successfully and in a way that will ALWAYS benefit you. Jesus loves you as no one else can, does, or ever will. His words, his promises...all of it are real. There isn't a phony or fake molecule in his being. And when you choose to give your life to him by filtering everything through him *first,* there is no possible way you will ever have to worry about anything fake or phony turning your life upside down. Even when those things try (which they will), Jesus is willing and able to stop them in their tracks. All you must do is get out of his way and let him.

Will you do that? Will you at least start by taking baby steps toward him?

Pray

Pray this simple prayer (or one like it) to ask Jesus to help you think and act based on the truth of his words (the Bible):

> *Jesus, I am not sure how to put all my trust in you, but I know I want to, so please help me. Forgive me when I mess up, and give me the courage to keep trying. I am thankful you love me no matter what, and I want to be able to give that kind of love back to you. I want our relationship to be authentic. Amen.*

Reality Check

Some of the most common reasons for not believing in or trusting Jesus all point back to one thing. EMOTIONS. They feel sad and mad because they didn't get what they prayed for. They feel scared and alone because people deserted, deceived, or abused them. They feel confused and disillusioned because they do not understand how a supposedly so good and loving God would allow bad things to happen.

Emotions fuel all these reasons. But you know how volatile our emotions are, don't you? Emotions are all over the map. They can change faster than the speed of light and go from one extreme to the other in less time than it takes to check your latest notification. Think about it—what emotions take over when watching a scary movie? Or a chick flick? Now, compare those emotions to *reality.*

The reality that...

Houses aren't haunted. No one is hiding in your attic, waiting to terrorize you. The popular girl never gives up her title of prom queen to the good girl who didn't rat her out for cheating on her science exam. The football team star with the best smile never ditches his equally trendy girl-friend to make the dream of the shyest girl in the school come true.

These things don't happen because the reality of human nature won't allow it. BUT the truth of Jesus' heart *is* 24/7 unconditional love and selflessness; it is the only way Jesus *can* be.

Jesus has already made his choice—a choice with no take-backs. And he chose you and me. Now it's up to you to make *your* choice. Do you want the most important relationship you'll ever have to be a relationship that time and history prove *cannot* fail? Or are you going to keep looking?

Mirror, Mirror...

Spend a few minutes to separate your feelings about Jesus from what you know (facts) about Jesus. How do the two 'lists' match up?

Now think about the things, experiences, and people influencing each list. Was there ever a time when someone or something else came through for you in a bigger or better way than Jesus?

Finally, think about two or three major decisions, situations, or problems you currently face. How will thinking and trusting Jesus to be better than feeling and impulsively reacting your way through these things?

2

THE BEST FRIEND ANALOGY

Greater love has no one than this, that someone lay down his life for his friends.

— JOHN 15:13 ESV

You probably know your mom and dad's best friends pretty well. You've probably spent a significant amount of time with them and like being around them. You might even consider them as a bonus, mom and dad. But it is impossible to be as close and connected to these people like your parent(s) are because these relationships have been built over time and the sharing of life experiences, hopes, dreams, fears, joys, and everything in between. One thing you *can* get from these relationships is inspiration and understanding how to *be* and *have* a best friend.

You will also learn that a best friend is someone who knows you inside and out—for better or worse—and sticks around anyway. Oh, and a best friend always has your back, no matter what. Best friends are one of life's greatest treasures. They are also part of God's design.

God created us to be relational. He knows friends are essential. He knows having best friends is important and wants us to have them. But God doesn't just know we need best friends; He possesses every quality necessary for *being* that friend. He's the best of the best. His ability to be a best friend can't be equaled or beat. In other words, **Jesus wants to be your best friend, and you need to want him to be yours.** Why? Because he...

- Created us, which means he knows us better than anyone. Even better than we know ourselves.
- He will never turn his back on us and never do anything to hurt us. Think about it—do you know anyone who doesn't guard their work...their creations...their masterpieces with their life? Exactly!
- Has known and loved us like no one else can since the beginning of time. Since before we were even born.

You aren't going to find anyone more qualified than that!

Reality Check

When choosing your best friends in the people department, time, life experiences, and similar interests you share, make many choices for yourself. But when it comes to your relationship with Jesus, he has already chosen you to be his BFF. No, seriously, he can be everyone's best friend and *still* be the best of the best.

He's been 'putting in the time' and sharing your life for all your life. All you must do is choose him back. He doesn't expect you to be all-in right from the start. He knows it will take time. But choosing Jesus as your best friend is the best choice you will ever make. It's worth every nanosecond you spend choosing Jesus over anything and everything else.

Mirror, Mirror...

Take a few minutes to read the following Bible verses about friends and friendships and ask yourself how your relationships fit into each one.

Now reread the verses and think about how things would change for the better by choosing Jesus to be your best friend.

Iron sharpens iron, and one man sharpens another. ~Proverbs 27:17 ESV

Do not be deceived: "Bad company ruins good morals." ~ 1ˢᵗ
Corinthians 15:33 ESV

Therefore encourage one another and build one another up, just as
you are doing. ~ 1ˢᵗ Thessalonians 5:11 ESV

Oil and perfume make the heart glad, and the sweetness of a friend
comes from his earnest counsel. ~Proverbs 27:9 ESV

Above all, keep loving one another earnestly, since love covers a
multitude of sins. Show hospitality to one another without
grumbling. As each has received a gift, use it to serve one another,
as good stewards of God's varied grace. ~ 1ˢᵗ Peter 4:8-10 ESV

Pray

When you pray today, thank Jesus for choosing you to be his best friend and ask him to help you decide to make him yours.

3

FINDING YOUR TRIBE

A friend loves at all times, and a brother is born for adversity.

— *PROVERBS 17:17 NIV*

K aty and Elizabeth's friendship started in second grade, and even though they both had take-charge personalities, they rarely argued or disagreed about anything. But they started drifting apart when Katy began playing basketball in junior high, and Elizabeth, who cared nothing about sports, didn't. Elizabeth suddenly found herself feeling like an out-of-style sweater.

It wasn't like she didn't have other friends. She had her friends from church and her 4-H friends, but she and Katy had always done things together until they didn't.

Elizabeth spent the first semester that year feeling miserable. But when the school nurse started a program for students interested in going into nursing (which Elizabeth was), Elizabeth found a new tribe. Girls and guys she had known most of her life went from being just kids in her class to actual friends—people she had things in common with and who enjoyed the same things she did.

Elizabeth and Katy weren't enemies. But when they didn't care about the same things, the bond they once shared started fading away. It happens a lot—especially when you are in junior high and high school. You don't mean for it to happen. It just does. It doesn't mean you love that person less or they love you less. It's just part of life. It's not your fault.' We are constantly evolving, meeting new people, and growing our circles. Trust me; you'll save yourself many days and nights wondering what you did wrong, why 'nobody' likes you anymore, and being angry at someone trying to figure out all the same things you are. A wise friend told me, "You can never have too many friends. The number of friends you have reflects the size of your heart." If you are closed off and try to force your friend circle to be smaller, you are confining your heart and potentially ignoring the blessings coming your way. Just be your true authentic self, keep growing, and keep your heart open and you will make friends wherever you go, and blessings will continue to flow.

Remember what you read a few pages back—how God created us to need and want friends? So don't worry about it. Pray about it. Ask God to put the people in your life whom he *knows* you need...and who need you. You'll know who they are when they show up. You'll know because they will be the people who like and love you for who you are, with whom you have things in common, *and* who respect and appreciate your differences.

Reality Check

Remember when you first started playing with your friends when you were little. Are any of those people still your friends? If they are, why are you still friends? If not, why did the friendship end? Or did it just sort of dissolve slowly?

Mirror, Mirror...

Make a list of the qualities you think are most important to have in a friend.

Take a good, long look at the list when you are done. Do YOU bring all of those qualities into a friendship?

Think about the people in your tribe. Chances are, the differences in your personalities and your different abilities do as much for your relationship as the commonalities. What do you think?

Pray

Read Luke 6:31 in your Bible and use the following thoughts to help you pray for your friends.

- Ask God to feel confident and sure that you are choosing the friends He wants you to have.
- Ask God to help you appreciate your friends for who they are.
- Ask God to help you notice when your friends are feeling sad or upset and let them know you care.
- Ask God to help you treat your friends the way you want to be treated.
- Ask God to help you choose friends who will never expect you to disobey Him.

4

HOW TO CONNECT WITH GOD

Draw near to God, and he will draw near to you. Cleanse your hands, you sinners, and purify your hearts, you double-minded.

— *JAMES 4:8 ESV*

I f you read through the verse above quickly, it sounds a little harsh. It almost sounds like a challenge. It's not. But it *is* a conditional statement. You might recall that term from English class. But just in case...

A conditional statement has an if...then condition. If 'this' happens, then 'that' will happen, too. Or if 'that' is true, then 'this' cannot be.

So, what James is saying is that when YOU decide to get close to God, He WILL move closer to you. But since God cannot associate or be close to those with a sinful lifestyle, getting close to God means giving up anything and everything He says is sin. In other words, you can't have it both ways. You can't be close to God and keep doing things you know are wrong (Exodus 20). That's what being double-minded means.

When it comes to God, it's all or nothing. You can't just show up in church, sing the songs, give all the 'right' (churchy) answers, and then spend the rest of your time doing life on your terms. That's nothing more than knowing *about* God...the end.

Do you remember a few pages back when we talked about knowing your parents' best friends—how you know their names, what they look like, where they live, and things like that? You know who they are, and you know a little (or maybe a lot) *about* them, but you don't really *know* them. You don't know how they think, how to discern their moods and feelings, and how to connect with them. You don't know these things because you haven't made the investments of time and personal interest (sharing the good, bad, and in between of life) with them. Well, guess what? The same is true when it comes to your relationship with God.

If you want to genuinely connect with God, then you must make yourself completely available to him. You must be transparent and 'all in.' You have to...no, you *get to* be completely honest and open with God. In return, you are going to A) have the best friend anyone could ever imagine, B) get rid of a lot of emotional and even physical baggage that was weighing you down, and C) you will be able to see, think, and do life better. You won't be struggling to know your purpose, what should come next, and all those other things we stress over when we aren't going to the right place (person) to get the answers.

You need to know, though, that making this all-important connection with God doesn't mean you aren't ever going to mess up or make mistakes. It doesn't mean all your troubles are going to disappear magically. But it does mean that you will not be battling these things on your own. God will be the one in the lead, fighting for and with you. Everyone sins, messes up, or makes mistakes at some point in our lives. God knows this. He created us to be this way. We serve a merciful Lord that is never mad at you and will always forgive you when you ask Him to. This is the beauty of repentance. Repentance is when we recognize the faults of our actions, take ownership of them, and ask for forgiveness. That is where growth happens.

That's what a real connection with God is, what a real relationship with God does for you.

Reality Check

Sounds great, you say. But how? How do you get to that level of closeness with God? In the same way, you get to the level of best friend status with the best friends you hang out with. Make God a priority. Try these suggestions:

1. Create a prayer routine. Don't start your day without talking to him and listening to what He has to say to you. This happens when you pray and just spend time being quiet to let the message of the thoughts God wants you to think come into your heart and mind. Praying is talking to God; meditation is listening. You need both talking and listening in any healthy relationship. Try getting into the habit of praying with a small meditation each morning as soon as you wake up.

- Every morning I wake up and get on my knees to pray with my arms open wide, with thankfulness being the central theme of my prayers. After my prayer and small mediation, I make my bed and start the day. This routine helps me start the day feeling centered and grounded.

2. Establish a Bible reading routine. Routines are great; it takes the guesswork on what to do next out of the equation. I'm sure you brush your teeth and hair around the same time every morning. Routines help you get out the door on time. So why not do the same when it comes to giving God the time He deserves and that you need to get to know Him better? To

really know Him. Start with something you know you can do—say, five minutes in the morning and five minutes at night.

3. There is something tremendously powerful about starting your day in gratitude. Here is an example, "Dear God, thank you for waking me up this morning, for the roof over my head and the food in my mouth, thank you for all my friends and family, and for loving me the way you do. I live a blessed life, and it's all because of you. Guide my thoughts, words, and actions and help me be whom YOU want me to be today. I am ready to seize the day." Thank you, Jesus. Amen.

Be patient with yourself and with God. Don't beat yourself up for not always "getting it right." God doesn't. Your practice does not have to be pretty or perfect. It's not about that. It just comes down to a little bit of discipline and a whole lot of love. And don't forget, God knows just what you need when you need it, and all those other details, so trust Him enough to let Him do things His way. You won't be disappointed. Not ever.

Mirror, Mirror...

Put your Reality Check plan down on paper and start incorporating it as a part of your day... an essential part of your day. Even more important than breakfast (but don't skip that, either). You do not need to know exactly what to think, say, or do. Remember, it's not about that. It's about setting the intention, and it's about love. You can always write your morning prayers down in a notebook and read from that. This helps you organize your thoughts; eventually, it will all flow naturally.

Pray

Pray for help to stick to your plan of connecting with God so that He will become the center and most important in your life. Pray for courage and determination to put God first and to make your connection with Him solid, strong, and your number-one priority in life.

5

PEACE WITH GOD THROUGH FAITH

But God demonstrates his own love for us in this: While we were still sinners, Christ died for us.

— ROMANS 5:8 NIV

Okay, Jesus paid the penalty for everyone's sins by dying on the cross. But why? It was an act of love, that's why. But why do God and Jesus love us that much? Because...

- God IS love. (1ˢᵗ John 4:8 and 1ˢᵗ John 4:16)
- We are all created by God and made in his image, which means we all have a piece of God's spirit in us.

(Genesis 1:26-27) And since God is love, it would be impossible for him not to love himself or anything that is part of Him.

That's huge! It's more than we can fully wrap our heads around. But that's okay. We don't have to understand it all. We just believe it. That's not being gullible or naïve. We do it all the time with things a lot less critical. For example, do you know every step it takes for the combustion engine of your car to operate? Until now, did you even know it was a combustion engine? Or do you know the routes the wiring and plumbing take in your house to give you high-speed internet and a hot shower? Yet you still trust these things to work whenever you want to use them.

So why can't it be...why *isn't* it the same when it comes to trusting and believing that God and Jesus love you enough to want to be with you always and forever, no matter what? Even if you don't understand it all (which none of us do), you can still believe it, accept it, and reap the blessings that come from it. That's what faith is and what this is all about.

Faith is why you believe and why you pray. Faith is why you read and obey the Bible. Faith is why you choose God. Faith is why you don't have to wander around lost.

Reality Check

How many things do you do on' autopilot' throughout the day or week? You have no problem putting your trust and faith in them, so why not do the same with the creator and maker of all?

Mirror, Mirror...

Is an aspect in your life blocking your vision from putting your complete faith in God? Is it disbelief? Are you afraid of being made fun of? Do you feel guilt and shame in your life? Have you been hurt by someone you should have been able to trust, making it hard for you to trust anyone? God is grander than any of these things. He can work through and round them all to show you how real His love is. Relinquish control over anything blocking your way and open your eyes and heart so you can see.

Read the following verses about the reality and bigness of God's love. Let God's words override any doubts you have. Let them convince you that His love is eternal and that wondering *why* is nothing more than wasted energy. Just take Him at His word and know God loves you.

Give thanks to the God of gods, for his steadfast love endures forever. Give thanks to the Lord of lords, for his steadfast love endures forever. ~Psalm 136:2-3 ESV

Nor height nor depth, nor anything else in all creation, will be able to separate us from the love of God in Christ Jesus our Lord.
~Romans 8:39 ESV

The steadfast love of the Lord never ceases; his mercies never come to an end; they are new every morning; great is your faithfulness.
~Lamentations 3:22-23 ESV

Pray

This is a prayer to God to help you never doubt His love for you.

> *God, the Bible tells me that your love doesn't fail. It says you are faithful and will never turn your back on me. Help me to release any fear I have that is blocking me from fully accepting your love. It seems impossible, but when I stop and think about the way you have already worked in my life, I know anything is possible through you. But I need you to help me stay focused—not to doubt and not forget. In Jesus' name, amen.*

6

SPIRITUAL BLOCKERS

The Lord is my strength and my shield; my heart trusts in him, and he helps me. My heart leaps for joy, and with my song, I praise him.

— *PSALM 28:7 NIV*

I've lived in Florida for eleven years now. The humidity and the hot sun are just a way of life here. Every dermatologist would agree that sunscreen is an essential step in every morning skincare routine, regardless of age or gender. It's important to block those harmful cancer-causing rays while still soaking up the natural vitamin D.

Have you ever fallen asleep on the beach? The gentle waves sing you a lullaby and the sun is a warm blanket on your skin. Sounds so relaxing, but after an hour, you wake up and realize you forgot to turn over, so you are red on one side and pale on the other. Do you have someone in your life that wears socks on the beach? Come on. Everyone seems to know one person. Their ankles, where the light never touches, are ghostly pale.

All Christ wants to be is the bringer of light into your world. He doesn't wish to leave anywhere unseen. We do not want any spiritual tan lines. We can see and feel a noticeable change in every aspect of our lives that we allow Christ to come in, whether it's our finances, our hopes and dreams, anxieties and fears, or relationships. Christ is the light of our life, but he is also the ultimate shield.

But you, Lord, are a shield around me, my glory, the One who lifts my head high. ~ Psalm 3:3

What is "the spiritual sunblock" in your life preventing you from having that more profound relationship with God? What is spiritually blocking you from connecting to the Holy Spirit inside you? Is there an aspect of your life you need to relinquish control over and allow God to take over? Is something taking up too much time and energy preventing you from spending quality time with the Lord?

Mirror, Mirror...

Part A)

Write down anything that you would consider a spiritual blocker in your life. It could be a toxic relationship, too much social media, not spending enough time in church, or even fears about the future. After being honest with yourself, start by setting realistic goals and taking baby steps to eliminate those spiritual blockers.

Part B)

Go for a walk and talk with God. This is one of my favorite prayer methods. Go for a walk outside and have a conversation with God. Talk to Him about anything you have going on in life. God is interested in every single aspect of your world. After your walk, write down any thoughts or ideas that came to you in your prayer journal. These are a gift from God. Don't forget to wear your sunscreen!

Pray

Dear Jesus, I want to be close to you. I want to feel your presence in every aspect of my life. Soften my heart and reveal to me any spiritual blockers in my life that could be preventing me from giving all of myself to you. I relinquish control because I have faith in You and want your will for me, not mine be done. You lift my head high in confidence, Lord. Through you, I know I can accomplish anything. You are my refuge and my shield; I have put my hope in your word (Psalm 119:114). In Jesus' name, Amen.

7

YOU CAN'T DRINK...OR POUR FROM AN EMPTY CUP.

"The most important one," answered Jesus, "is this: 'Hear, O Israel: The Lord our God, the Lord is one. Love the Lord your God with all your heart and with all your soul and with all your mind and with all your strength.' The second is this: 'Love your neighbor as yourself."

— MARK 12:29-31 NIV

The second most important thing Jesus told us to do is *'Love your neighbor as yourself.'* This means you are supposed to fully embrace yourself for precisely who you are in this very moment, to truly love yourself, and yet the self is often the most forgotten, or this self-love concept is regarded as selfish. When Jesus tells us to love our neighbors as ourselves, he says we cannot fully love anyone without loving ourselves first. Let's talk about self-love.

What is self-love? Glad you asked.

Dr. Jeff Borenstein described it this way: *"...Self-love means having a high regard for your own well-being and happiness. Self-love means taking care of your own needs and not sacrificing your well-being to please others. Self-love means not settling for less than you deserve."*

Another explanation of the meaning of self-love says this: *Loving yourself doesn't mean you think you're the smartest, most talented, and most beautiful person in the world. Instead, when you love yourself, you accept your so-called weaknesses and appreciate these so-called shortcomings as something that makes you who you are. When you love yourself, you have compassion for yourself... You take care of yourself as you'd care for a friend in distress. You treat yourself kindly. You don't nitpick and criticize yourself."* *~Andrea Brandt, Marriage/Family Therapist*

No one could argue that these aren't accurate definitions of self-love. Knowing *what* it is, isn't the problem. Believing it's more than okay to love yourself and knowing *how*—that's the hard part, especially in this season of life.

The bombardment by all forms of media, well-meaning adults, and even people who are supposed to be your friends can make it a struggle. Think about it—when Olympic medalists like Simone Biles, Nancy Kerrigan, and Kathy

Rigby all admit to suffering from depression or eating disorders because of the pressures put on them about their weight and shape, something is wrong! These girls' bodies have done amazing things, yet in the eyes of people who don't matter, they still were made to feel like they weren't good enough.

Girls, listen up! Loving yourself is more than just okay. Loving yourself is a command from Jesus!

The verse everyone is most familiar with is Psalm 139:14. You may know from memory, but just in case... *"I praise you because I am fearfully and wonderfully made; your works are wonderful, I know that full well." (NIV)*

I almost didn't use it here because it is used so often. But I did because of what Christian author and speaker Darla Noble said when using this verse. "Do you believe the Bible is true? Then you must believe this is true about YOU because God made you, and God don't make no junk!"

Say that last part with me now: GOD DON'T MAKE NO JUNK!!!!!

Reality Check

True statement: You are exquisite and YOUnique. God made you in His image with true love and intention because God has a plan for you. You are not the only one to question how or even if this is true. Job did, too. And when he did, God didn't waste any time setting the record straight.

Then the Lord spoke to Job out of the storm. He said: "Who is this
that obscures my plans
with words without knowledge? Brace yourself like a man; I will
question you, and you shall answer me. Where were you when I
laid the earth's foundation? Tell me, if you understand... Have you
ever given orders to the morning...Have you entered the storehouses
of the snow
or seen the storehouses of the hail, which I reserve for times of
trouble, for days of war and battle? Or shown the dawn its place..."
~Job 38:1-4, 12, 22-23 (NIV)

This goes on for *five* more chapters! God made it perfectly
clear to Job that His personal investment in creation is
intense. Spoiler alert: Job receives the message loud and
clear...

Then Job replied to the Lord: "I know that you can do all things; no
purpose of yours can be thwarted. You asked, 'Who is this that
obscures my plans without knowledge?' Surely I spoke of things I
did not understand, things too wonderful for me to know." ~Job
42:1-3 (NIV)

That is not to say you don't have a responsibility to care for
what He made, aka YOU. You owe it to God and to yourself
to treat your body—inside and out—with dignity and TLC
by making wise choices when it comes to exercise, eating a
healthy diet, getting plenty of rest, setting personal
emotional and physical boundaries, refusing to let anyone or

anything harm your body (that includes you). Your actions, words, and attitude must show the world that you know you are valuable because God made you, and GOD DON'T MAKE NO JUNK.

Mirror, Mirror...

Ask yourself the following questions:

1. Can you answer 'yes' to the following question without hesitation, "Do I love myself?"
2. What three things do you love most about yourself? What three things do you love least about yourself?
3. Who or what has the most influence over you regarding how you see yourself as a person—inside and out? Are they positive or negative influences?
4. List three things you will do daily that fall into the category of 'self-care' that will remind you of just how special you are?

FYI: If you are engaging in dangerous and harmful behaviors like drinking or using drugs or suffering from eating disorders, anxiety, or depression, if you have thoughts about taking your own life, or are the victim of any form of abuse, please, *please* know that you are too valuable and precious to be hurting in these ways. Stop now and ask God to open your heart and mind to the hope He offers and give you the courage RIGHT NOW to ask for help.

Pray

Dear Jesus, help me feel confident and assertive, comfortable in my skin, and know that I am special and unique. Help me to love my whole self for who I am in this very moment. Through you, I know I have so much to offer the world. I give all my negative thoughts to you. Help me remember that feelings and emotions are not the same as truth and knowledge—the truth and knowledge in the Bible that says I am one of a kind—a unique masterpiece made by God. Thank you. Amen.

8

SHHH... MAYBE SHE'S BORN WITH IT?

Beloved, if God so loved us, we also ought to love one another. No one has ever seen God; if we love one another, God abides in us, and his love is perfected in us.

— *1 JOHN 4 11-12*

You may recognize the title from the old Maybelline make-up commercials, but in this context, we're not talking about an artificial glow; we're talking about the ultimate glow. The Goddess light of the Holy Spirit that you are reborn with after accepting Jesus into your heart as your Lord and Savior. When you have genuinely decided for yourself to be a follower of Christ and turn your will over to the care of God, your old life is shed away, and a rebirth into the new takes place. Proverbs 1:23 is a promise from God saying that if you choose to turn towards Him, He will pour His spirit into you. The Holy Spirit helps us be called whom we are supposed to be. This is our God conscious, our inner God compass that points us away from sin South and straight towards the true North. When situations arise, with practice, you'll get better at noticing when your God-conscious is trying to tell you the decision you need to make.

If no one has told you today, let me start by saying, "Girl, you are beautiful, inside and out, exactly the way you are at this very moment! No matter what you have going on, hair up in a messy bun, braces, maybe a few pimples, or no make-up. It doesn't matter. You are gorgeous and worthy of being loved and accepted, just as you are right now in this very moment.

God knew what you would look like inside and out before your parents even met.

Say the following out loud:

I am a beloved child of God.
God help me to love and see me the way you see me.
I know I am worthy of love, just as I am right now.
I know that you love me just as I am right now.
I know I am accepted just as I am right now.
I know that you accept me just as I am right now.

Write these affirmations on a sticky note and place them in your mirror. Recite it every time you brush your hair or your teeth. This is also an excellent exercise for any Bible verse you are trying to memorize.

When you believe without a shadow of a doubt that God loves you and that a piece of the mighty God dwells inside you, you will be able to embrace yourself as you are without judgment and reservation. Also, when you believe God loves you, His love will flow effortlessly from your heart to others. This will help you to purely love everyone else around you, knowing that God also dwells inside them. If you want to be a lover of people as God is, by faith, simply embrace the fact that He loves you! How we treat people is evidence that we know God.

Mirror, Mirror

I will let you in on one of the secrets to feeling more beautiful. It's not expensive make-up or a rigorous skincare routine; just two words: Give Compliments.

Get in the habit of giving at least three sincere compliments a day without any expectations of getting one in return. By doing this, you are taking the focus off yourself, and you start actively looking for the goodness in others. Here are my three to you.

1. I love the way you think.
2. You have a great smile!
3. I love how kind you are.

9

I FEEL JUST AWFUL ABOUT THAT, BUT WHAT CAN I DO?

Therefore, as God's chosen people, holy and dearly loved, clothe yourselves with compassion, kindness, humility, gentleness and patience.

— *COLOSSIANS 3:12 (ESV)*

Sixteen-year-old Zach was the number one runner on his high school's track and cross-country teams, setting unbroken records for over a decade. But what made Zach stand out was how he stood on the sidelines cheering on his teammates. Especially Arden—the guy who always finished last.

One day, Zach's compassion and respect for Arden went above and beyond. It was a cold, rainy day. Not a heavy rain —just enough to make you miserable. It was the last event— the mile. Zach finished in barely over four minutes. Arden was on his third lap (of four) at just over six minutes and was the only one still running. But Arden, who had never let that stop him, kept going. But this time, Zach went back on the track instead of just cheering him on and started running beside Arden.

"What are you doing?" Arden asked.

"Running," Zach said with a grin.

"Why?" Arden asked.

"Because I thought you'd like some company. And if I'm going to have to get wet, I may as well be doing something other than standing around," Zach said, winking at Arden. "So, let's do this."

Arden didn't run any faster than usual, but he ran with more confidence, and he finished knowing that at least one person didn't think he was a complete loser.

That, my friend, is compassion. Seeing someone in pain and doing what you can to make it better. Feelings of lostness, loneliness, or worthlessness are natural feelings that unfortunately creep into even the happiest of people. Most people can relate to at least one of those feelings. If you know a friend suffering, have compassion and understanding and reach out to them. Give them a call. The phone can be heavy when you're in the thick of those emotions. Do your best to help because you know those are all lies the enemy loves to tell. Sometimes all someone needs is an ear that will listen.

Jesus was the master of compassion (along with a lot of other things). His compassion led him to give blind people their sight, cure people of the dreaded disease of leprosy, let people who had never walked take their first steps, and even gave parents their children back by bringing them back to life. But here's the thing—Jesus' compassion wasn't a perk, so to speak, given only to people who followed and believed in him. It was compassion in its most authentic and sincerest form—wanting to make things better and doing whatever he could to make that happen.

Did everyone on the receiving end of Jesus' compassion put their faith and hope in him? Did everyone who benefitted from Jesus' heart change their ways and beliefs and accept him as their Lord and Savior? No. We know from reading Luke 17:11-17 and Luke 7:26-37 that people who benefitted from Jesus' miracles—directly and indirectly—weren't always grateful enough to give Jesus what he wanted most. Their faith. What he enjoys most from us is simply our faith in him (Luke: 36-50).

Reality Check

What about you? Where does your compassion come from? Are you genuinely concerned, or are you more about looking good? Is it about doing things to put on your college application essay? Making you more popular? Winning votes for prom queen or student council? Feeling pressured to keep up your family's image or reputation?

Don't be too quick to answer. Be honest with yourself and with God. Even the most minor bits of selfish or wrong motives have the potential to turn compassion into 'not compassion.' That doesn't mean sadness and empathy are the only right reasons for offering support. Sometimes justifiable anger moves you. This refusal to stand on the sidelines and let injustice win causes people to be compassionate. For example, people who donate to charities, prepare homeless survival kits, volunteer their time and talents to a shelter for abused women and children, or adopt a puppy rescued from a puppy mill are showing compassion because they are justifiably angry about the situation or want justice to win.

It's also not always going to be something big (like the examples you just read). For the most part, the little things make the most significant impact, like running alongside the lonely runner. When you give generously from the heart, you have the power to change someone's life completely. Never doubt the potential impact that you may have by blessing someone else with your time. God can work miracles with very little. Just like the boy with the few loaves and a couple of fish (John 6). All you need to do is have faith; the impact of your compassion and generosity could spread to thousands.

Mirror, Mirror...

Read Luke 10:25-37 and Genesis 45:1-8. After you are done reading, take a few minutes to list some things you can and will do over the next few weeks to show compassion for people—both those you know and those you don't know.

Pray

Start asking God to give you opportunities to show compassion for others. But be ready because God will not hesitate to answer you. Be prepared to hear and see the openings He sends you. And do not be afraid to act. Remember—God will never ask you to do something He did not think you were more than capable of handling.

10

I WANNA BE ME, BUT FIRST I HAVE TO FIGURE OUT WHO 'ME' IS

So then you are no longer strangers and aliens, but you are fellow citizens with the saints and members of the household of God.

— *EPHESIANS 2:19 ESV*

Back in 2000, i.e., before any of you were born, Jessica Andrews released a song that was a huge hit. The song's title was *"Who I Am."* Part of the lyrics go like this...

*I am Rosemary's granddaughter; The spitting image of my father; And when the day is done My momma's still my biggest fan. Sometimes I'm clueless, and I'm clumsy, But I've got friends that

love me, and they know just where I stand. It's all a part of me, and
that's who I am....

Whatever genre of music you listen to, you've gotta love this song because she's a girl who isn't afraid to admit and embrace who she is. She knows herself and respects herself. She knows where she comes from. She knows that she can be a hot mess sometimes and owns it. Ske also knows she always rebounds to be just who she is...no matter what.

Some of you get exactly what she's singing about. You know where you come from, who you are, and have a solid set of people who love you no matter what. For some of you, this could be a goal you are striving towards or something you'll add to your prayer requests. And some of you are somewhere in the middle. But everybody wants what she has. Everybody.

The problem with that is the enormous pressure put on you to have already all this figured out and neatly in place. There is the internal pressure you put on yourself. Plus, all the external pressure. Societal pressure places unrealistic demands and expectations on you to *know exactly* who you are *and* want to be.

This is supposed to be a fun and exciting time in your life! Appreciate this season of your life by making lifelong friendships and being fully present when spending family time. Also, take this time to discover and explore anything it is that you think you would like to learn. Maybe you've always wanted to learn how to draw, play guitar, or take a pottery class. Enjoy learning all about you and your God-given talents without fear or judgment. When we fail to try because of fear of what others might say, we prevent ourselves from living up to our full potential. If what you are trying to learn is not your thing or makes your heart sing, that's ok too! I congratulate you for trying and stepping out of your comfort zone. Move on to something else and keep spreading your wings.

You have the power to turn the pressure around. You can turn the stress and uncertainties weighing you down into a platform of resilience and faith. How? By making truth your number-one go-to source of information and encouragement.

Reality Check

- Genesis 1:27 says you are created in the image of God.
- Galatians 2:20 says that those who have accepted Jesus as Lord and Savior have the Holy Spirit living in them. That means you are never alone. The Holy Spirit is a part of you.
- Jeremiah 29:11 says that God has specific plans for YOU. You are a girl with purposes and missions to complete.

- 1st Corinthians 6:19-20 is a reminder that it's not all about you. It's actually all about God; by respecting yourself, you are showing respect to God.
- 2nd Timothy 1:7 says the Holy Spirit gives you the power to be bold and brave.

Mirror, Mirror...

These four exercises will help you feel grounded and ready to seize the day!

1. Look in the mirror and say, "I am a strong and capable young woman; I can accomplish anything I set my mind to."
2. Do not start your day without asking God to help guide your thoughts, words, and actions and help you live up to your full potential. Then do your best to do just that.
3. Walk away from anyone who doesn't love and respect you for who you are—for your strengths and weaknesses. You don't need toxic people in your life or your space. You only have so much energy and time during the day. You deserve a safe space around you to be your most authentic self.
4. Memorize Psalm 56:3-4: "When I am afraid, I put my trust in you. In God, whose word I praise." (NIV)

Pray

Whenever you are not sure about what to do or say, ask God for help. You don't have to bow your head, close your eyes, or even say it out loud. God hears us even when we don't speak. Oh, and remember—He will never ignore you.

11

WHAT IS HAPPENING TO ME?

Do you not know that your bodies are temples of the Holy Spirit, who is in you, whom you have received from God? You are not your own; you were bought at a price. Therefore honor God with your bodies.

— 1ST CORINTHIANS 6:19-20 NIV

At this point in your life, you've also sat through a few science classes just for girls on how your body works, why you have hairy armpits, why your face is breaking out, and why you shouldn't worry if your friends get their period before you do. Hopefully, you also have a mom (or maybe a grandma) who has taken the time to have 'the talk' with you about sex. Not just the physical stuff about sex, but the emotional and spiritual stuff, because no matter what anyone tries to tell you, the emotional and spiritual sex stuff is just as important as the rest of it.

No matter how open the lines of communication are between you and your mom, there are probably still a few things you are unsure about. It's not easy to hear your parents, your youth pastor, or the preacher at church saying one thing while the media or some of your friends say another.

Oh, and let's not forget about hormones! All the crazy things that happen to our bodies happen (for the most part) because of hormones. SIDENOTE: You probably already know this, but just in case you need a reminder, hormones are chemicals that carry messages back and forth to the different organs in our bodies.

Sounds simple and innocent enough, right? Not! Sometimes our hormones either get ahead of the rest of our body or fall behind. When these things happen, which can often be, we start thinking and acting weird. We cry about everything. We get mad for no reason. We can't concentrate in class. Our egos are easily bruised. We convince ourselves we are ugly, fat, hopeless, and the biggest loser ever. We ghost our friends because we think they are holding us back or get paranoid that they are ghosting us. We do dumb things to get attention. Then we either beat ourselves up for whatever it was we did, or we blame anyone and everyone but ourselves for our actions.

It's a vicious cycle but one you don't have to ride.

Reality Check

God created hormones just like He created everything else. You need to know that there are lots of things you can do to keep your hormones under control. 'Under control' doesn't mean they won't go crazy occasionally, but when you treat your body the way God made it to be treated, you will be dazed and amazed at how much better you think, act, and feel.

That may be hard to believe sometimes, but it's true. Look...

- Who you are from the inside out really is more important. *Charm is deceitful, and beauty is vain, but a woman who fears the Lord is to be praised. ~Proverbs 31:30 (ESV)*
- We are supposed to be different from one another. *Just as a body, though one, has many parts, but all its many features form one body, so it is with Christ...Even so, the body is not made up of one part but of many. Now, if the foot should say, "Because I am not a hand, I do not belong to the body," it would not for that reason stop being part of the body. ~1st Corinthians 12:12-15 (NIV)*

- God is personally invested in you. *But now, O Lord, you are our Father; we are the clay, and you are our potter; we are all the work of your hand.* ~*Isaiah 64:8 (ESV)*
- When things get crazy, just ask Jesus to help and relinquish control over the situation. Jesus will help soften your heart, guide you in the right direction, and improve everything. *Let us then, with confidence, draw near to the throne of grace, so that we may receive mercy and find grace to help in time of need.* ~*Hebrews 4:16 (ESV)*

It's true! God is personally invested AND interested in YOU!

Mirror, Mirror...

1: Are you in the habit of talking to Jesus? That's what prayer is, you know. You can speak to him like he's your best friend because that's exactly who he wants to be...Jesus is supposed to be your best friend.

Starting today, I want to challenge and encourage you to spend five to ten minutes a day talking to Jesus. This could be included in your prayers out loud or written down in a prayer journal. Tell him what's on your mind. What's bothering you? What's on your heart that no one else understands? What scares you? Your goals, hopes, and dreams. Ask him to open your heart and mind to what he wants. Do not be discouraged from asking Jesus for guidance on anything you have going on in your life. Ask Jesus never to let you forget that not even hormones can get you down when he's in charge.

2: Take care of yourself. Are you eating a healthy diet (primarily fresh food with no chemicals, dyes, and processed sugar)? Are you getting at least forty minutes of exercise a day? How much sleep do you get every night? What about drugs and alcohol? Those are a hard no. How much time do you spend online or listening to music, and would you be embarrassed if Jesus or your grandma were in the same room when you do these things?

There's probably room for improvement in at least one area. Make a list of what needs to be changed, decide how you will make that happen, and then start getting it done.

3: Have you ever heard the line, "Secrets don't make friends."? It's true. You need someone to confide in. Someone to talk to about your acne that refuses to clear up. Someone to talk to about guys. Or that overwhelming feeling of being unable to breathe because of the pressure to get accepted into a particular college.

Don't choose just anyone to share your secrets with. Choose an adult you can trust. One who loves you like no one else except God. Hopefully, that someone is your parents or grandparents. It's also okay to have a friend to confide in, too. But when it comes to getting answers you can trust and the ones you need to base your choices and decisions on, you need to go to someone who has experience. Someone who wants the best for you spiritually, physically, and emotionally. Someone who will do whatever it takes to love you through these struggles. If your mom or grandma is not a possible option (which I know is sometimes the case), pray for a spiritual mama from your church— may be the mom of a Christian friend, a youth leader, or a Bible teacher can be a trusting ear.

12

STOP COMPARING YOUR BLESSINGS

Give thanks in all circumstances, for this is the will of God in Christ Jesus for you.

— *1 THESSALONIANS 5:18*

E ver find yourself scrolling on Instagram or Facebook only to start feeling low and contemplating if you are doing enough in life? That FOMO starts to really kick in, doesn't it? I think we've all been there. The deceiving part is that we only see the most highlighted, golden moments of life, not the hardships it took to accomplish that feat. You didn't see the hours of working overtime to make that family trip happen or the insane amount of hard work it took for a friend to receive the acceptance letter on your feed.

Have you ever seen someone give a presentation and thought, "Wow, she is crushing it! I wish I could speak with that much confidence, clarity, and grace in front of people." You did not witness the panic attack the night before, the amount of praying she did right before she went on, or the several hours it took to prepare the material. We only see the results, not the miracles that transpired in the shadows.

I struggled with this in high school and college. I tried to keep up with the latest fashion trends instead of developing my style. I compared my average grades to other classmates and allowed resentment and jealousy into my heart. Jealousy and resentment are a manifestation of fear. The root cause of this fear comes from the notion that we think we lack something, the lack of creativity or lack of intelligence. The vicious cycle of constantly comparing creates a tunnel vision that blinds you to the abundant blessings that God has provided (James 3:16). Instead of focusing on the negative, the truth is that God's love has provided me with warm clothes to wear and put people in my life that could be of assistance.

The opposite of lack is abundance. If you truly believe God will provide and always has your back, you will never lack (Jeremiah 29:11). Just have faith that the Good Shepard is leading you down the perfect path for you. I'm not saying I never catch myself slipping into comparing my situation to others. But I have trained myself to nip it, return my mind to a place of gratitude and focus my attention on my blessings and the path that God has led me down.

Every hill and valley of life is an opportunity to rely on Jesus and deepen your personal connection with Him. He is with you in the shadows, and He is with you in the light. Praise Him during your victories and lean in during your times of growth. Embrace the season you are in and see the miracles God is doing in your life.

Just like each of our life paths is unique, so is our relationship with God. We must learn not to compare our spiritual relationship with God to someone else's or think we have a Bible study routine that is better or not enough. Throughout this book are exercises for you to do to help deepen YOUR personal relationship with God. Find which methods you vibe with the most and focus on those. If you are reading this book with a friend, maybe their favorite way is writing in their prayer journal at night, and yours is a walk and talk with God. That's great; I'm thrilled! That is a success story because two people have found their own personal ways to connect with God.

Reality Check

Living your life in a constant state of gratitude has the power to alter your vibration and how you see the world completely. It's all about your perspective and how you view the world around you. God is with you in the mundane tasks of the day; He wants to be there. Everything we do is an opportunity to give thanks and appreciation. Instead of saying, "Geez, I can't believe I have to do the dishes again," try saying, "I *get* to do the dishes." Instead of fussing over all the laundry to fold, try thinking, "Look at all these beautiful, clean clothes I get to take care of." This changes our outlook from being full of complaints to a perception full of gratitude. When we switch our perception to a state of gratitude, our internal glow burns brighter. Our confidence increases and the love for ourselves and everything around us grows, eventually attracting like-minded, positive, appreciative people into our world. God is in the middle of it all, constantly blessing us, even while we're doing the dishes. It's up to us to open our eyes and see it.

Mirror, Mirror...

1) Who do you compare yourself to, and why?

Has anyone ever compared you to your siblings? A teammate? How did these comparisons make you feel?

Take a few minutes this week to think about who you are—what makes you, you. After you've done that, think about your best friend. Are you two an exact match? Probably not. But that doesn't make one of you better than the other. Your differences *and* your similarities are what make you friends.

2) The next time you feel a FOMO spiral coming on, or you find yourself feeling a little anxiety about the future, or possibly a painful memory creeps in, try this:

Recenter yourself to the present moment through a few deep breaths. Return to a state of gratitude. Take a moment and meditate on the many blessings in your life. Breathe in the gifts of your life and breathe out in appreciation.

Write down three things you are grateful for today and consider telling them to someone else. Spark an appreciation conversation and spread the loving feeling of gratitude.

Before bed, list all the things you are grateful for, big and small. You can write something like your parents and clean running water to drink and brush your teeth. This exercise helps you clear the mind, focus on your many blessings and resize your problems. You'll be able to sleep at ease knowing that God is always with you and provides what you need when you need it.

Pray

God, I want to be my most authentic self, the way I know you meant for me to be. Sometimes it isn't easy. I want to break all habits of comparing my blessings to others right now. I am so grateful for the life I live today. I am so thankful for my family and my friends. I truly live a blessed life. Help me take care of my body and not be embarrassed or afraid to be Me. In Jesus' name, amen.

WHICH WAY WILL YOU CHOOSE?

Jesus said to him, "I am the way, the truth, and the life. No one comes to the Father except through me.

— *JOHN 14:6 NIV*

It hasn't been all that long ago that people had to depend on maps and road signs to reach their destination. Well, that *and* their ability to read and follow them. No GPS. No voice coming from their phone saying things like, "In 3.2 miles, use the far-left lane to turn left onto...." But somehow, they managed. They managed just fine because A) they knew it was their only option, and B) they trusted that neither the maps nor the signs would lead them somewhere they didn't want to go.

That's the way it is with Jesus...only following Jesus is wayyyyyyyy more critical than any map or road sign. And the destination he leads, which is the promise of heaven, is a wayyyyyyy better destination than anyplace else you'll ever go.

But why follow Jesus? And why did he have to die to get back to heaven and make it possible for *us* to get there someday? Why not have some sort of punishment or penalty system in place?

Answer: Because nothing we could ever do would be enough to cover our debt...to make up for the sin in our lives. But God loves us too much to let that keep us apart.

We sin, and God cannot be associated with sin. His holiness won't allow it. And by 'allow,' I mean it isn't possible. The two cannot exist in the same place, just like you cannot set water on fire. But God loves us *so much* that the thought of not spending eternity with us was heartbreaking. That's right. We mean that much to God.

That may be hard for you to believe, but it's true. God created each of us for himself and didn't want to give us up. Look...

> *"...everyone who is called by my name, whom I created for my glory, whom I formed and made." ~Isaiah 43:7 NIV*

"I, even I, am he who blots out your transgressions for my own sake and remembers your sins no more." ~Isaiah 43:25 NIV

For by him, all things were created, in heaven and on earth, visible and invisible, whether thrones or dominions or rulers or authorities —all things were created through him and for him. ~Colossians 1:16 NIV

So...

Because God and sin cannot mix, and God's love for us is so overwhelmingly immense, He knew he had to provide a perfect and sinless way to bridge the gap. And that way was Jesus. Jesus, God in human form, was perfect and holy in every way, so God offered Jesus as a payment for the world's sins. It was His gift to both Himself and us. It wasn't easy, but love isn't always easy.

Reality Check

Here's something to think about...

Jesus was willing to die for you and everyone else in the world (past, present, and future), knowing that countless people would not fully understand. They may not accept God's gift on His terms, which are faithful obedience to Him out of love and gratitude. That's ok. Jesus did it anyway and would do it again even if it were just for you.

Think about that for a minute or two.

Now think about this:

FACT: You have the freedom to choose whether to give your life to God and live life on his terms.

FACT: God has known who will and won't accept his gift of Jesus' payment for their sins since the beginning of time.

FACT: He did it anyway.

Mirror, Mirror...

Have you accepted Jesus' gift of salvation? If not, what is stopping you? If you have, are you living a 'thank-you' kind of life, i.e., living life on God's terms? What can you do today to take your faith and obedience to the next level?

Pray

Spend a few minutes thinking about how scary and hard it must have been for Jesus to be nailed to the cross. He did it anyway, so think about how much faith he had in his Father, God, to go through with it. It helps you realize the level of love God and Jesus have for us, doesn't it? So, please take a moment of gratitude to thank Jesus for what he did. He rose again so we could have life. Ask for forgiveness for the sins you have done and for the courage to be more like him.

14

A LITTLE FISH IN A GREAT BIG OCEAN

Remember your leaders who spoke the word of God to you.
Consider the outcome of their way of life and imitate their
faith.

— *HEBREWS 13:7 (NIV)*

It took Christina a few minutes to figure out where she'd seen the lady there to speak to her FCA (Fellowship of Christian Athletes) club. When it finally came to her, she knew the lady wouldn't remember her but decided she needed to tell her how much that week had meant to her....

"Hi," Christina said shyly. "I know you don't remember me, but I remember you."

"Really?" the lady asked, apologizing for not recognizing Christina. "From where?"

"From a church camp. I was in sixth grade. I lived at Show-Me Christian Homes. My house parents were the mission-aries at the camp that week. I was in one of your Bible classes. I remember the lessons you taught—especially the one where you spit in the pudding." Christina started laughing.

"Oh, wow!" the lady laughed, too, and then smiled. "That's so special that you remember the lesson...and me." Then she reached out and gave Christina a little hug and grinned. "I hope you remember *why* I spit in the pudding."

Christina said she did. "I was baptized the Sunday after we left the camp, and the next year I came to live here with my aunt and uncle. Anyway, I just wanted to say thanks, because your lessons were great. I'll never forget them."

The lady started crying at that point. "Now look what you've done," she teased Christina. "I'm going to be a mess standing up here talking to you all."

You might not be surprised that she didn't give the talk she'd prepared. Instead, she told the rest of the group about the conversation with Christina. She used it to remind them that even though we feel like little bitty fish in a gigantic ocean, God's always got his eye on us and protects us. He is our ulti-mate protector and provider. She also reminded them that even though we might not think what we say or do matters, it does because someone (like Christina) is always watching and listening.

Reality Check

The Bible doesn't leave any room for doubt about Jesus being the one you need to follow. In John 14:6, Jesus says he is the way, and no one comes to God except through him. The book of Acts (4:12) states that there is no other name but Jesus by which we can be saved. But that doesn't mean God doesn't put people in our lives to teach, mentor, and love us so that we can strive to become more like Jesus. Jesus' last words on earth included telling us to 'make disciples,' which means to help other people want to become Christians, too. Helping each other become more mature Christians isn't an option; it's part of our life purpose as Christians. It is something Jesus commands and expects us to do. But you are responsible for letting this happen. You must be willing to be mentored and taught. Are you?

When you think about it, why *wouldn't* you want more mature Christians in your life? You don't depend on your little brother to help you with geometry; no one would even consider asking a sixteen-year-old to teach a defensive driving course. So why not make sure you learn from the people God has placed in your life?

Mirror, Mirror...

Who are your leaders? Whose faith and the Christian way of living do you respect and admire? Let them know these things. Tell them. Send a card or email. Thank them for setting a solid example.

Whom are YOU leading? Don't say anyone because your friends and siblings are watching you even though you may not realize it. They want to know if this 'God stuff' is for real. They want to see if you are who you say you are. I know —it's a big responsibility. But you need to know that it is a responsibility you aren't dealing with alone. Living your life *for* God guarantees that you are living with God, and He will never leave you hanging.

Pray

> *God, please help me choose my mentors wisely. Give me the courage I need to reach out to the right people. Please give me the opportunities and experiences I need to meet like-minded individuals who are also seeking to know you more. I do not want to do life alone. I know I need people, and I entrust you to place the right people in my life for every season. I want to surround myself with people who love you, God. In Jesus' mighty name, Amen.*

15

WHAT WAS GRANDMA ALWAYS SAYING ABOUT SPICES?

Even in the case of lifeless things that make sounds, such as the pipe or harp, how will anyone know what tune is being played unless there is a distinction in notes?

— 1ST *CORINTHIANS 14:7 (NIV)*

This scripture reminds me of the old saying, "walking to the beat of a different drum." We are all born with unique talents, gifts, and our own tune. These days it takes courage to fully embrace your differences and be truly happy for someone else's skills. Thank goodness we do not have to be perfect at everything to enjoy life. It takes the pressure off and allows us to focus on our blessings and appreciate the gifts of others.

I know girls who can take down a deer with a shotgun better than most guys I know. I know girls who would rather spend their time hiking, sleeping under the stars, and eating meals cooked in tinfoil over a campfire. I know girls whose idea of enjoying nature goes no farther than listening to the sound of rain on their phones while getting their nails done in 'sky blue' or 'rose petal pink.' I know girls who like curling up with a good book and a latte and girls who would rather have waffle fries.

Who's the real girl in all these? Answer: All the above! So, to answer the question, the title of this chapter asks, "What was Grandma always saying about spices?" the answer is that variety is the spice of life.

Aside from the fact that it would be unbelievably dull if we were all the same, you need to remember that we are ALL created in the image of God, meaning we all have bits and pieces of His character. But because God is so...so...*everything* good and wonderful, He doesn't create everyone with the same 'pieces' of him. The Bible mentions this several times—especially in the New Testament. In 1st Corinthians chapters twelve and fourteen, Romans chapter twelve, and 1st Peter chapter four, Paul talks about how we are all different but ultimately have the same purpose—to make sure whatever we do honors, God. In the Old Testament, we read about God blessing certain men with gifts and talents in construction, music, sculpting, and carving, serving as legal authority, counsel, and full-time ministry.

All these people were the same in how their bodies were formed and functioned. But *who* they were—that's what made them different individuals. Exactly how it still is today.

Reality Check

Why do you wear your hair the way you do? What made you think you had to have that pair of Crocs, Air Forces, or Vans? If that's truly your style, that's fantastic; keep rocking it. Trying to keep up with the latest trends is like a never-ending hamster wheel.

What extracurricular activities do you do after school? Does it bring you joy, or are you participating because of outside pressure?

Sadly, some waste so much time and effort wishing for and trying to be someone they are not. It also hinges on cutting away at God's holiness. Remember a few chapters ago when I reminded you that God *"don't make no junk?"*

When we focus on obtaining more possessions to make us happy and solve our problems, we will always come up short, feeling empty and low. Don't get me wrong—it's not a sin to wear makeup, dress fashionably, or have more shoes than your dad thinks you need. Just be your true authentic self. Enhance your unique flavor and groove to your beat. That is what makes you cool! Happiness is a fleeting emotion. Do not count on anything other than your relationship with God to make you joyful and complete. Jesus is the best role model in the universe. Strive to be as Christ-like as possible, and you will live a fulling life.

Mirror, Mirror...

Do something 'crazy': go through your closet and get rid of anything that isn't 'you.' If it doesn't fit right if you're not vibing with it anymore, or it was a Christmas present from two years that you've never worn, donate it! Decluttering is so satisfying.

16

SOME DAYS ARE BETTER THAN OTHERS

The steadfast love of the Lord never ceases; his mercies never come to an end; they are new every morning; great is your faithfulness.

— *LAMENTATIONS 3:22-23 (NIV)*

My dad passed away when I was five. I will never forget him and never stop loving him. But I also love my other dad—the man who raised me. He and my mom got married four years after my biological dad died. At first, it was weird because I was used to just being me, Mom, and my little sister. She doesn't even remember our dad because she was just two when he died. But Dad didn't come in and try to take over everything. He expected us

to obey him, but he wasn't pushy and didn't try to change every-
thing. Becoming a family was a process, and he and Mom worked
hard to make sure we knew how thankful they were that God had
brought us all together. And you know what? I am, too. ~Felicia
(17)

My mom is the most positive person I know. It's annoying some-
times. Sometimes I just want her to let me whine and complain
without telling me how thankful I should be. I don't want her
always telling me to look for the good in things...and then making
a list of all those good things. Sometimes I need to vent without her
making me feel guilty for feeling bad. Is that too much to ask? As
long as I don't stay stuck in pity-city, isn't it better to be honest
about my feelings? God knows what I'm feeling, anyway, so isn't it
a little bit like lying to ignore or deny what I'm thinking and feel-
ing? I'm not like my mom that way. Sometimes, or even most of the
time, I need to take a different approach to work through things. I
know I have a lot to be thankful for, and God knows what he's
doing, but that doesn't mean I always have to like it. Does it?
~Audrey (15)

It isn't always easy to be thankful—especially when you have
a rotten day. You know, the day when your hair is frizzy,
someone throws up on the bus, your pen leaks out on your
sweater in an awkward place, and you sneeze so hard during
debate practice that snot comes out your nose. No way are
you thankful for days like that!

Those things are rough. But not as harsh as a lot of the days
Moses had. He spent forty years leading through the blis-

tering hot desert despite all the whining, complaining, and sometimes defiant Israelites. Yet he still managed to thank God for everything God did to keep them safe and provide what they needed. One day, though, Moses had had enough. The people were complaining (again) about being thirsty. They were 'sure' God was going to let them die. This had happened once before, and God, true to his word, had provided water to drink. From a rock, no less! So, he decided to do it again.

Now, the first time God used a rock for a drinking fountain, he told Moses to hit the rock to get the water going. The second time, though (Numbers 20:2-13), God told Moses to say to the rock to send out water. Moses was in the habit of obeying God to the letter. No one can argue that. But on this particular day, Moses was at his breaking point with those ungrateful Israelites. He had had it 'up to here! So, instead of telling the rock to provide water for them to drink, Moses whacked the rock with his staff. Water flowed, and the people drank it and stopped complaining (for a while). But what ended up being a good day for them turned out to be the worst day of Moses' life.

God was so upset with Moses for disobeying Him that he told Moses he would not be allowed to go into the Promised Land. He could see it from a distance, but he would not be allowed to take the last leg of the journey. Moses wouldn't be allowed to finish what he'd so faithfully and humbly started and executed.

That's a bad day. But nowhere do we see Moses whining, complaining, or trying to talk God into changing his mind. We don't see it because it's not there. Moses couldn't have been happy about God's decision but accepted it anyway because he trusted God's holy and perfect character. He knew this was part of God's divine and perfect plan for the universe.

God didn't hold a grudge toward Moses. He didn't keep reminding him about the way he'd messed up. He continued to bless Moses in many ways, to love him, and trust him to lead the Israelites to the boundary lines of the Promised Land. That was enough for Moses because he knew a vital lesson we all need to learn—a little blessing from God is more significant than the biggest, most valuable thing we might ever receive from anyone else.

Reality Check

Some of you have had excruciatingly hard days. Days when the word 'bad' doesn't even begin covering what's happening. Some of you have lost parents to cancer. Some of you have gotten that phone call telling you your family pet is very ill. Or maybe your worst day ever is having to move out of the house and town you've lived in your whole life. Let's be honest and say that being the new girl in the middle of the school year isn't easy, no matter what grade. Or maybe your worst day is breaking your leg the day before cheer tryouts or standing on stage on the opening night of the school play and forgetting your lines. Or even worse, taking too many steps stage front and falling off into the orchestra pit.

There is no way to put losing a parent or being the victim of an abusive parent on the same playing field as not making the cheer squad. BUT at the same time, you need to remember that: a) it's not a contest, b) you should never feel like your bad day is not significant because it's not as sad or life-altering as someone else's, and c) no one's bad day is something God can't handle.

Accept God no matter how bad, sad, tragic, or scary. Please do not harden your heart and throw your faith out the window. God will comfort you, protect you, and heal your brokenness (Psalm 23:4).

Mirror, Mirror...

How would you complete this sentence: The three worst days of my life were....?

How did you handle them? Who did you go to for help? Whom did you lean on? And most importantly, how much time did you spend sharing it all with God and asking Him to get you through it?

I'd like to say your worst days are behind you. I can't do that because none of us has the power to see the future or control the choices and decisions other people make. But what I *can* tell you is this: when you put God at the top of your go-to list and when you trust Him always to have your back and know what is best for you, those awful, horrible days that make you want to crawl under the covers and never come out, won't be that way forever. God *will* work things out somehow, some way. He will give you plenty of things to smile about, look forward to, and be *thankful* for.

So go ahead—don't be shy. Ask for what you need and want, and then be ready to say 'thanks' when He answers. Oh, and don't ever think God isn't listening or doesn't care because He is, and He does.

Pray

God is no different from any parent when it comes to needing to know that we appreciate all He does for us and that we trust Him to know what is best. Tell Him about these things during your prayer time each day.

17

YOU WANT ME TO DO WHAT?!?

Remember the Sabbath day to keep it holy. Six days you shall labor and do all your work, but the seventh day is a Sabbath to the Lord your God. On it you shall not do any work....

— *EXODUS 20:8-10A (ESV)*

'Sabbath'—now there's a word for you. It's definitely not one you will find on your vocabulary test (if you still have vocabulary tests). You are also not going to hear it in a movie or on a television commercial. And I promise you will never be asked, "Do you have any objections to working on the Sabbath?" on a job application. So, what is it? What is the Sabbath, and what does it have to do with you?

Question one: The Sabbath is the day God set aside for resting and focusing your attention on enjoying 'God stuff.' Rest from what? From everyday work and activities. What kind of God stuff? Worship, church, fellowshipping, and just being glad God loves you. And one other thing about the Sabbath—God didn't suggest it. He commanded us to observe it.

Question two: What does the Sabbath have to do with you? Everything, really. And here's why…

Fact #1: God created us. He put every muscle, blood vessel, and hair in place. He chose your eye, skin, and hair color and the size of your nose and ears. He decided who your parents would be if you had food allergies and whether you would like to read or not. In other words, God knows more about you and your needs than you do. He knows the intimate details of your past, present, and future. God also knows when you need to rest and has the ability and authority *to make you* rest, especially if the way you live is unbalanced.

Fact #2: God will help you rest physically and mentally. He knows what will keep us working at an optimum level. Read Psalm 23: 2-3.

"He *makes me* lie down in green pastures, he leads me beside still waters, he refreshes my soul. He guides me along the right paths for his name's sake."

Lying on green pastures beside quiet waters sounds so relaxing. Think of your mind as the calm waters. Generally, during the week, it is a rushing river. You need to give your mind a break from all the rushing for your mental health. FYI: This reason alone should be enough to make us *want* a Sabbath day.

Fact #3: Observing the Sabbath is a command—not a suggestion, remember? Without the Sabbath, we don't allow our bodies and minds to focus on and do the things God created us to do. Our human nature is to constantly stay busy, which ultimately keeps us feeling further and further away from God.

Fact #4: You need the Sabbath. I need the Sabbath. We all need the Sabbath.

Reality Check

Most people think the Sabbath is about sitting around doing nothing. No work of any kind. No fun of any kind. An entire day to sit around, think of God, and read your Bibles. That's not what the Sabbath is meant to be.

The Bible gives us a different impression of the Sabbath. And since the Bible is…the Bible, it needs to be the only source we rely on and follow. We'll examine a few things the Bible tells us about the Sabbath. Some of the verses listed below tell us why God gave us the Sabbath. Some tell us what Jesus and his disciples did on the Sabbath. Some instruct us on how to use (do) the Sabbath…and how not to.

- Mark 2:27 The Sabbath day was made for you and me for us to take of ourselves.
- Then God blessed the seventh day and made it holy because, on it, he rested from all the work of creating that he had done. - Genesis 2:3
- Hebrews 4:9-10 A Day out of the week is dedicated to rest from all work precisely the way God created the Universe.
- Luke 4:31 Jesus himself taught on the sabbath. The scripture explains how Jesus performed a miracle in front of the congregation. He simply removed an impure spirit from a man by giving it orders.
- Acts 18:4 Describes the Apostle Paul preaching on the sabbath, trying to spread the word of Jesus to potential new believers.

When you read these verses, you'll start to notice a pattern—that the Sabbath was part of every Israelite's weekly routine. A day to calm the mind and body and nourish the spirit. Remember to stay present and refrain from going on autopilot. These days it's not so much about doing the Sabbath wrong. These days, 'doing' Christianity *without any sabbath* is the problem. It is a problem because not observing a Sabbath is in-your-face disobedience to something God commanded. It is a problem because we need rest for our mental and physical health. We've already established that. A third important reason for a rest day is that real growth happens in the stillness. When we take the time to slow down and meditate on the word, that is where the more profound connection with God is matured.

Mirror, Mirror...

How many extra-curricular activities are you involved in? How much sleep do you get on average? How much time each day (yes, each day) do you spend just 'being'—no screens, no homework, no organized and structured events? Do you take the time to clear your head, dream dreams, rest, spend time with God, read a good book, take a walk, or bake your favorite cookies...?

We all need a day each week to do the things that quiet us, make us feel rested, and turn off the busy, rapid-fire stimulation in our heads. None of those things are necessarily bad, but when they are *all* we think about, or when they crowd God to the back of the line, they become destructive.

I also want to ask you this: How many house rules have your parents given you that you consider optional? Or ignore them altogether? Just askin'....

18

YOU CAN MAKE A DIFFERENCE

"You are the salt of the earth, but if salt has lost its taste, how shall its saltiness be restored? It is no longer good for anything except to be thrown out and trampled under people's feet. "You are the light of the world. A city set on a hill cannot be hidden. Nor do people light a lamp and put it under a basket, but on a stand, and it gives light to all in the house. In the same way, let your light shine before others so that they may see your good works and give glory to your Father who is in heaven."

— MATTHEW 5:13-16 (ESV)

S alt and light—are two everyday, ordinary things everyone has and uses. You don't think much about them. They are just there. You flip the lights on and off in your house without wondering if they will work or not. You don't even consider the possibility that the saltshaker might be empty or that the fries you ordered won't already have salt on them.

Have you figured out where this is heading?

He is sending us a beautiful message by comparing us to two common and essential things. Yes, salt is indeed a necessary compound for the body. Jesus is sending two messages. Message One: No matter how ordinary and small you may feel in this Universe God created, Jesus wants you to know that you are extraordinary and an essential piece of it. You are responsible for loving people as Jesus loves and telling people about the gift of salvation available to them. This has the potential to create generational spirituality. Message Two: Lead by example. Your unconditional love for Jesus and people will continue to flourish. This love is the infectious light described in the scripture. Your love and kindness will reach far and wide and spill over to everyone you meet. Through your interactions and the way you speak, coming from a place of love, people will feel it and receive blessings just by being around you. This will enhance the spirituality of your community. It all starts with you. You are essential and have the authority to make a massive impact.

When you read your Bible or hear about the people labeled heroes in the Bible, you need to remember that they were ordinary people just like you and me. The only difference between them and you (besides the way they dressed and their unusual names) is that they chose to say yes and let God use them.

Reality Check

Today is another one of those days when you are going to do some serious thinking about your relationship with God. More specifically, you will spend some time thinking about how YOU can be a little (or a lot) saltier and shinier when it comes to letting people know what you think about Jesus and his role in your life. To get you started, take a few minutes to read the following verses. After you finish reading the 'Mirror, Mirror...' this section will help you organize your thoughts and decide what your next move will be.

1. Colossians 4:5-6: Walk in wisdom toward outsiders, making the best use of the time. Let your speech always be gracious, seasoned with salt, so that you may know how you ought to answer each person. (ESV)
2. 1 Timothy 4:12 Let no one despise you for your youth, but set the believers an example in speech, in conduct, in love, in faith, in purity. (ESV)

3. Hebrews 13:16: Do not neglect to do good and to share what you have, for such sacrifices are pleasing to God. (ESV)

4. Proverbs 3:5-6: Trust in the Lord with all your heart, and do not lean on your own understanding. In all your ways, acknowledge him, and he will make straight your paths. (NIV)

Mirror, Mirror...

Reading these verses with the mindset of thinking about the things you *should* do and what you *should* say is the critical first step toward being the difference maker God created you to be. Thinking about these things isn't enough. You...me... we *all* need to *be* proactive. *Be* **salt and light.**

So...what are you going to do? What do the words from the verses you just read say to YOU about making a difference in your family? Among your peers? In your school? On your campus? On your team? In your community? In your church? On your social media? Think about it, pray about it, and do something about it.

Pray

Have a heart-to-heart conversation with God about being a difference-maker. Don't worry about admitting you are scared. He knows it. Don't worry about telling Him you don't feel like you can do anything that matters. Have courage. He knows you can and is super-excited to prove you wrong (in a friendly way, of course). After you are done spilling your guts to God, get comfy, get still, and listen to what He has to say back to you.

19

F-O-R-G-I-V-E-N-E- S-S

For if you forgive other people when they sin against you, your heavenly Father will also forgive you. But if you do not forgive others for their sins, your Father will not forgive your sins.

— *MATTHEW 6:14-15 (NIV)*

You don't need to read between the lines to get what is being said in these two verses, do you? But did you realize that these words came straight from Jesus? This is what Jesus had to say right after giving his tutorial on how to pray, which we call The Lord's Prayer.

Some people look at this and say this proves we must earn our way to heaven. Wrong!

Jesus' message (or warning, if you want to call it that) is simply saying that by not forgiving someone for their mistakes, you consciously decide to hold on to grudges and resentments. Grudges and resentments poison the soul and will eventually make you feel distant from God. This unforgiving mindset distorts your judgment, and your decisions are rooted in fear and anger.

For example, let's say you decided to walk down a different hallway in school because of a tizzy you had with a friend. Instead of facing the confrontation head-on and choosing forgiveness and love, you are taking the longer path and choosing to walk in fear and anger. Always take the shorter pathway to forgiveness and love.

First stop: What is forgiveness? Forgiveness is the *deliberate and conscious choice* to let go of hard feelings, resentment, anger, and grudges against someone, including ones you may have against yourself. Forgiveness is *choosing not to let* anger, resentment, hurt feelings, pride, and grudges control your thoughts, actions, and attitudes. Forgiveness is moving beyond and forward from painful and hurtful situations instead of allowing them to stifle your present and future happiness, confidence, and success.

Second stop: What *isn't* forgiveness? Forgiveness is *not* saying it is okay or acceptable that someone did something to hurt or deceive you. Forgiveness is also *not* ignoring these actions, pretending they are unimportant, or, when applicable, forgiveness is *not* taking the appropriate steps to hold someone accountable for their actions.

Third stop: How do you forgive? That's the hard part. It takes practice. When conflict occurs, it's common to get defensive instead of being humble and listening to the other person speak. That's where faith and your relationship with God come in. Forgive as you would want to be forgiven. I want to be forgiven promptly and gracefully without any leftover animosity, so that is what I'll strive to do for others.

Reality Check

Jesus didn't make any apologies or excuses for what he said about forgiveness, either. Why would he? Jesus didn't do anything that required anyone's forgiveness. Not ever! We certainly can't say that, can we? But thanks to Jesus, we do not have to pay an eternal penalty for our sins. We do not have to live with guilt or be ashamed of our mistakes. You do not have to keep tabs on everything you've done wrong. Let it go. Give it up all to God.

We are forgiven! Yes, everyone is exonerated of all things ever done wrong. But we must acknowledge and accept what Jesus did. Otherwise, it's useless. It's like going out into the cold, snowy weather without wearing the coat, hat, and gloves hanging right by the door. They are right there, ready for you to put on, but you decide not to for one reason or another. The decision to 'put on' Jesus' gift of salvation is way more important.

Forgiveness isn't just a nice thing to do or a good idea. It makes us more like Jesus. It moves us closer to God. More like Jesus…closer to God…what could be better than that?

Mirror, Mirror…

There are countless stories throughout the Bible of Jesus forgiving individuals for all kinds of mistakes (Luke 7:36-50). It is to help you realize that you can forgive someone for anything and everything. Nothing anyone does to you, or you may do to yourself, is unforgivable.

1) Make an amends list. Try this for any past or present conflict situations in your life, including ones with yourself. Write the problem all down. After praying over the issue, see precisely your role in the conflict. Is an apology necessary? Make sure to only apologize for your part in the incident and ask if there is anything you could do differently moving forward. Do all this without expecting an apology in return. Once you have gone through the list and made all the amends, let it go. Toss the paper in the trash and never look back.

2) Take a few minutes to look up the following verses about forgiveness. Think about each verse and how you can apply it to your life situations so that you

don't have to lose a minute's sleep over wondering if
God has forgiven you.

- Ephesians 4:32
- Matthew 18:21-22
- 1 John 1:9
- Colossians 3:13
- John 3:16
- Matthew 5:7

3) Anytime we feel angry, it is an opportunity to look
within. A chance to find stillness and truly analyze
where the feeling is coming from. Instead of being
reactive like yelling and shouting, we can automati-
cally learn to look toward prayer. We can look within
and discover the source and make peace with it. Why
exactly are you angry? Get specific. Ask God to
remove this from your life. These are opportunities
that God gives us to learn to listen to our God-
conscious. After prayer, we feel calmer and can better
handle any situation in front of us.

Pray

Confess any grudges and resentments toward anyone,
including any towards yourself to God. Tell God you know
you need to forgive them, ask Him to take the hard feelings
from you, and replace them with love and forgiveness and
the commitment not to let those old feelings creep back in.

20

THE BEST WAY TO DO LIFE IS TOGETHER

Two are better than one because they have a good return for their labor: If either of them falls, one can help the other up. But pity anyone who falls and has no one to help them up.

— *ECCLESIASTES 4: 9-10*

Human beings were never meant to live alone. We were destined to grow together and love each other. We were designed to uplift each other just as the scripture says when one falls. Dark days do happen. It's inevitable. When you know Jesus in your heart and surround yourself with people who genuinely love and care about you, the dark days will never consume you. God does not create victims.

You will be victorious. You will prevail, and you will be comforted. Healthy relationships are a significant key to living a joyous life.

What is happening around you is always a reflection of what is happening inside you. When you have love and kindness in your heart, that is what your world will look like. If you feel scattered and lost or your world seems chaotic and damaging, start with taking a long, hard look on the inside. Every single healthy and flourishing relationship begins with a spiritually healthy you.

Behold, you delight in truth in the inward being, and you teach me wisdom in the secret heart.
~ Psalm 51:6

When you take steps closer to God and ask Him to teach you about your heart, that is when the real growth begins to happen, God will reveal and shed light on places in your heart you never knew existed. That is what David means in the outward expression of love he shares in this Psalm. God knows your inward being and wants to reveal any pain you may have hidden in the secret catacombs. You may have judgment or shame that has been stored deep down into the catacombs of your being for so long that it becomes a part of you. Your body and mind conform around it and creates scars, wounds only partially healed. God will teach you how your heart works, and through this healing comes wisdom.

Jesus can heal any scar. If Jesus can heal the blind, he can heal your heart.

God speaks through people. He uses people to send messages, teach, and comfort us. A lonely Christian is an easy prey. Psalm 23: 5 says, "You prepare a table before me in the presence of my enemies." Well, Hillary, I do not have any enemies. The enemies are inside the mind. If you are alone too often, your entire mindset could shift and become deceiving. "I haven't been to church in such a long time that I must not need it." "I haven't read my bible in so long that I probably wouldn't understand it." "I haven't talked to my best friend in days. She must not like me anymore." The negative thoughts start to compound, but you do not have to give in. You never have to stay alone. Choose God. Believe in Jesus. Reach out to someone you love and respect.

Leaning into God and understanding how much He loves you is the ultimate defense against the lies that try to weasel their way into your head. When you move your heart towards God, it does not just benefit you. Your relationship with your parents transforms, and your relationships with your friends and teachers also change. When you learn from scripture about how God loves people, you stop looking at peoples' faults and start seeing how God sees them with love (Philippians 2:5). You forgive easier, you have more compassion, and your love grows deeper. Only when you ask God to open your heart and actively pull the weeds away first will the fruitfulness of your soul shine and bless all your relationships (Mathew 13: 24-29).

Mirror, Mirror...

The first significant step in creating the relationships you want is that you need to know precisely what you want. What type of relationship do you want with your parents? Envision it. Would you like a more open line of communication with your parents? Then you need to start talking. Would you like for them to trust you more? Then you must trust them and consistently show them you are trustworthy. Do the same thing with your friendships. What type of friendships do you want? Do the secret heart work necessary and remove any blockages you may have. It starts with you; it begins with your vision. Create the ultimate vision board for your life, pray about it, then get to work.

Create a vision for your life. Do not be afraid to dream big God dreams for your life (Ephesians 3:20)! What do you want it to look like? Get specific. If God can create the universe in a whisper, He can handle any big dream you have. It's ok if your vision changes, but by creating an image and setting goals, you are taking an active role in your life. You are setting intentions and allowing God to work miracles in your life. If you allow life to happen to you, you will constantly be living in reaction to your surroundings instead of the creator of your surroundings.

21

DO YOU EVEN HAVE TIME TO DATE?

Above all else, guard your heart, for everything you do flows from it.

— *PROVERBS 4:23 (NIV)*

This book will not tell you if you should or should not date. That decision is ultimately up to God, you, and your parents. Did you know that nowhere in the Bible is a record of anyone dating? Husbands and wives were chosen for each other or chose one another. But nowhere is dating even a thing. The closest thing we find is…

- Jacob worked for Rachel's dad, Laban, so that he could marry Rachel. This did not turn out so well because Laban was such a jerk. But that's a story for another day.
- Joseph and Mary were engaged to each other, but no dating or courtship. Just engaged and married.
- Esther was chosen to replace the queen (which she did). But there was no dating—just a selection process.
- Samson picked a woman to be his wife, then sent his father to get her for him.

Not a word...zilch...nada...about dating. But marriage? Oh, God has plenty to say about marriage, husbands, and wives. He gives us an in-depth look into the lives of several couples, giving us various issues married people face. Some of them do it according to God's way. Some don't. Okay, you say, but marriage is not on your radar. Not for a loooooong time. Good, I hope not.

Does this mean you absolutely cannot date *and* be a Christian? No. But it *does* mean your dating experience should look and be a whole lot different than what the world tells you that you should do. Don't worry; you can still go to prom and be a Christian. You can still have a fantastic time and create unforgettable experiences at the dance with all your friends without the unnecessary pressures of an intimate date.

Reality Check

Here are some guidelines to follow and research to read before you even think about dating.

1. Pray about it first. You put God first in every other aspect of your life; new relationships and dating are no exception. Use the vision exercise from the previous devotional.

If you are to date, ensure the boy's values align with yours. Does he love God? Is he on a spiritual path to intimately know God too? Does he pray? Is the relationship rooted in Christ? What type of relationship does he have with his friends and family? If you've answered no or are unsure of any of those questions, the intentions behind the connection should be questioned and possibly reevaluated.

2. Whom should you date?

Plenty of outside pressures are trying to mold your opinion and tell you whom you should or should not date. Just know that it is okay to have a different view than your friends, teachers, and the mainstream media. We must always be willing to listen and understand how other people feel and respect their decisions. We pass judgment when we start labeling others sinful for their actions and personal beliefs. That is not living Christ-like. Jesus loves everyone no matter what, and we should too. Love, compassion, and understanding are what this world needs, and you can lead by example. God is love. If you are confused on this matter, always turn to the Word, and ask your pastor or youth leader to explain. Here are a few pieces of scripture for you to read:

- Leviticus 18:22 (ESV)
- Romans 1:26-27 (ESV)
- 1st Corinthians 6:9-10 (ESV)

3. Don't put yourself in a position to be tempted. Sex is not an option for anyone outside of marriage.

This isn't a non-Christian vs. Christian issue. Hormones, peer pressure, and natural desires do not discriminate between Christian and non-Christian teens. Spending time alone with a guy is never a good idea. Your grandma would describe it as playing with fire. And when you play with fire, eventually, you get burned. No argument can be made to support the idea that sex outside marriage is okay. The following verses are from God's Word on the matter.

- Hebrews 13:4
- 1st Corinthians 6:9-11, 13, 18-20
- 1st Corinthians 7:2, 9

According to the CDC, the number of teens getting pregnant has decreased steadily over the past twenty years. In 2019 research showed that about 16 teen births occurred in every

1,000 teens aged 15 to 17. That is a 4% decrease just from the previous year. The reasons are not completely clear, but for the most part, it seems that abstinence is the main reason for the drop. YAY.

That *is excellent* news. But it doesn't take away from the fact that 80% of all teen pregnancies are unplanned (no surprise there) and that 30% of teen pregnancies end in abortion. It also doesn't change the hard truth that in all 100% of teen pregnancies, the teen mom's life with a baby growing inside her changes forever. All 100% of these girls must live with the repercussions of their pregnancy. Repercussions include becoming a teenage single mom or facing extreme decisions like giving the child up for adoption, going through the traumatic experience of abortion, or the risk of serious complications.

If you are reading this today and have already decided not to wait until marriage, you must know that God still loves you. He is not mad at you; He is madly in love with you. Jesus took on the guilt and shame of this world on his back so you do not have to carry that heavy burden backpack your whole life. Take it off and lay it down before him. I want you to be safe. I want you to know that you are loved and do not have to continue being sexually active to feel love. Learn deeper into the Word, pray to God for guidance and fill any voids you may have with the light of Jesus. Every day is a brand-new day and a chance to transform your life.

4. Trust God

I will leave you with one last thought on this critically important decision. And this is it: if you trust that God's gift of salvation is genuine, and you trust that Jesus' death on the cross does cover the penalty for all your mistakes, then why would you even think about doubting that God won't let you know who Mr. Right is? When the time is right.

Just sayin'....

Mirror, Mirror....

Dating and getting to know someone new on an intimate level takes a considerable amount of time and energy. This investment of time and energy means you are selflessly sacrificing time and energy from your priorities for another person. Let's divide your day into pieces of a pie. Cut the slices according to how much time you spend doing them. This includes physical activities and spiritual. Things to have in your pieces are time spent in school, after-school activities like dance, soccer, and homework, spending time with family and friends, and quiet time with the Lord. You can get as specific as how much time you spend on social media.

You'll be amazed how quickly your pie fills up, and you'll be able to take an honest look at where your priorities lie according to how much time you dedicate to them. Be honest here. If you cannot be honest with yourself and God, then who on this Earth can you? Maybe some slices need to be shifted around to give more time and energy to others like family or bible study.

I might be going out on a limb here, but I have a strong feeling about your busy schedule of trying to live your best life and focusing on being the best version of yourself. You probably do not have time to squeeze in a boyfriend. Your priority slices must get smaller to do that, and with this exercise, you'll be able to see precisely what you'll be giving up.

Pray

God, dating is a massive thing to girls my age. I never realized that the Bible does not give accounts of anyone dating. I've never given it any thought. I know sex is supposed to be off-limits. Honestly, though, that's a huge relief. I just don't know if I can be strong enough to do this your way, so I need your help. It's a crazy world we live in. You know that but living in the middle of it all is hard. I want to do the right thing and live for you, so please help me stay focused and help me say no to the things I should say no to. In Jesus' name, amen.

"RAISE YOUR HAND IF YOU HAVE EVER BEEN PERSONALLY VICTIMIZED BY REGINA GEORGE."

– MS. NORBURY

Make no friendship with a man given to anger, nor go with a wrathful man, lest you learn his ways and entangle your-self in a snare.

— PROVERBS 22:24-25 (ESV)

D o you know where the title of this chapter comes from? Do you know who Ms. Norbury is and why she said what she did?

For those who don't know, Ms. Norbury is a fictional teacher in the movie "Mean Girls." As for Regina George? She's the fictitious leader of the mean girls. And by mean girls, I mean…well, you know exactly what I mean. We all do. Mean girls have been around for centuries.

Potiphar's wife (Genesis 39) was a mean girl (woman). When Joseph didn't take her up on her offer to have an affair, she lied and accused him of trying to rape her. She did it for revenge and to show him that nobody got away with telling her 'No.'

In 1Samuel 1:6, we meet another mean girl. Look…

Because the Lord had closed Hannah's womb, her rival kept provoking her to irritate her. (NIV)

The rival's name is Peninnah. She is also married to Hannah's husband. Weird, I know…and a stellar example of why husbands aren't meant to be shared. Other examples of mean girls in the Bible are Hagar (Genesis 16), Sarah, who isn't completely innocent, or Herodias (Matthew 14).

I can still remember the mean girls in our high school. So can a lot of other women—older and younger than me. How do I know? Because I asked, no one hesitated to tell me about the mean girls in their school for a second.

Mean girls are real because pride, jealousy, greed, fear, and low self-esteem are real. They are also the ingredients that go into making a mean girl. Yes, you read correctly. Fear and low self-esteem are oozing out of every mean girl out there. When you add those two things to the others, you get a toxic reaction—kind of like pouring vinegar on baking soda. They lash out however they can to make someone else feel at least as bad (hopefully worse) than they do. They won't admit it. Most of the time, they don't even realize it. They think their looks, their family's money, the clothes they wear, the house they live in, and all those other things are enough. They are too scared and confused to admit they aren't. So instead, they deny the emptiness they feel *and* try to fill the space simultaneously. It's a lost cause, but that doesn't seem to matter.

Reality Check

When you stop to look at the mean girl syndrome from this perspective, it doesn't make sense, does it? It seems like a girl would realize what is happening and do something different to solve the problem. But let's face facts—it is always easier to see things more clearly when looking in on the outside. At least, I hope that's where you're at. I hope you are not a mean girl. More importantly, if you are a Christian, you had better not be...you cannot be a mean girl.

You cannot be the girl who rolls her eyes or gives the 'don't even think about talking to me' look to the new kid in school or those labeled as nerds, geeks, or any other stereotype title. You cannot be the girl who makes fun of someone's clothes or hair, who laughs at someone's awkward moments, who is rude, disrespectful, and unkind to anyone for any reason.

On the flip side, if you ever have been, currently are, or someday become the brunt of a mean girl's jokes, attentions, or comments, you cannot let it get to you. You must know that no one else's definition of you matters more than God's. No one else's perceptions and beliefs about you count more than God's. Is this easy? Positively not! But it *is* possible because God has equipped you with everything you need to make it possible—the number one resource being Him. His Spirit is living in you. I know you think you need more than that—something or someone you can see, hear and touch, but that's what faith is. Having faith is knowing that the Spirit *is* enough.

Mirror, Mirror....

This is the moment of four truths.

Truth #1: How do you treat others? Do you give them the grace to be themselves, make mistakes, embrace awkward moments, and celebrate wins? Or not.

Truth #2: How do you respond when you witness someone being victimized by a mean girl?

Truth #3: How susceptible are you to someone else's ideas and perceptions about you? To what lengths are you willing to go (or have you gone) to either disprove them or live up to their expectations for you?

Truth #4: Where does God fit into all of this in your life? More specifically, where do you let God fit into all of this?

Pray

Ask God to empower you to see others the way He sees them. Ask the Holy Spirit to drown out all the hurtful words, the self-doubt they cause, and the lies the world tries to disguise as truth. And don't forget to ask God to fill you with His goodness and to put a hand over your mouth whenever you are tempted to say anything unkind to anyone.

STAYING FOCUSED IN A WORLD OF DISTRACTIONS

Finally, brothers, whatever is true, whatever is honorable, whatever is just, whatever is pure, whatever is lovely, whatever is commendable, if there is any excellence, if there is anything worthy of praise, think about these things.

— PHILIPPIANS 4:8 (ESV)

Distractions are everywhere. They swirl around in your head. They jump out at you on the screen. They whisper like gossip. They scream like your three-year-old cousin when she doesn't get her way. They do whatever it takes to get your attention, taking it away from whatever was there first. Sometimes that's a good thing—like when the smoke alarm goes off in the kitchen because you forgot about the cookies in the oven. Sometimes, it's a bad thing—like hearing the notifications vibrate on your phone when you're trying to study.

There is so much noise in this world. The news. Music. Social media. School. Television. Your teachers and counselors. Your parents. Your friends. Your peers. The countless noises that are made by doing ordinary things. No wonder you don't always know who or what to listen to! It's also no wonder that you are not always sure who or what to believe and trust. No matter what, you know you can always trust and believe in God.

The book of Ecclesiastes says that everything old is new again. That history repeats itself. I tell you this to remind you that the distractions you have competing for your attention are not all that different from those your parents, grandparents, and other people way back when had to deal with. Teenagers have been hounded to choose an intelligent career path since the revelations. Music has been sending subliminal messages for centuries. The media has always had sneaky ways of telling us what's the latest fashion trends and how to wear our hair and makeup. The news has been telling us what we should think and how we should believe for decades.

Yes, every generation has its brand of distractions. But they also have something else. The remedy. And THAT has never changed. Not since the beginning of time. The cure for distractions has always been and always will be Jesus.

Reality Check

The reality of negative distractions is this: If you allow them to consistently draw your attention and focus away from God and His blessings, they have the potential to lead you astray and make you feel discontent.

The other reality is that God does not force Himself to be the center of our lives. It is up to you to keep your focus on God and off of everything else that does not serve a higher purpose. Does that mean you can't listen to music? No! But it does mean you can't listen to music with lyrics that disrespect God and His Word. Does it mean you can't confide in your friends? Or that you shouldn't take the advice of teachers and counselors? No! But it does mean you should always weigh what they say against God's Word and choose God's Word over anyone else's. Does it mean the news, social media, and other things should go? No! But keep cautious and keep God in focus.

Mirror, Mirror...

Spend time looking up each of the following verses and jot down a few thoughts on what each one says to YOU about staying focused on God.

- Psalm 119:15
- Psalm 19:14
- Matthew 6:33-34
- Hebrews 12:2

Instead of picking up your phone first thing in the morning, try picking up your Bible. Read just one verse. That's it, just one. You are deliberately choosing to put God first in your day. It also delays the instant dopamine rush of gratification you get from your phone and allows your brain and body to wake up naturally, thus giving your phone less power over you and your thoughts. Before bed, try reading just one Bible verse instead of mindlessly scrolling. This helps you to meditate on God's Word as you fall asleep. By getting into this habit, you give God the first thought in the morning, and the final say to end your day.

In what ways can you limit your distractions on each given day? I removed all notifications except text messages from my screen. This helps me stay present throughout the day and helps restrict my social media to only specific times during the day. I also only follow inspiring, uplifting, and encouraging pages. My pastor recently said this, and I think it drives home the message of social media and our phones, "If you do not control your phone, your phone will control you." Your God-given time is so precious. Focus on what truly matters.

Pray

Start each day asking God to help you stay focused on Him. Throughout the day, silently repeat that same prayer. Don't worry—God hears, and He answers.

HOW DO YOU SPELL "GROWNUP"

When I was a child, I spoke like a child, I thought like a child, I reasoned like a child. When I became a man, I gave up childish ways.

— *1 CORINTHIANS 13:11 ESV*

Children shouldn't be made to grow up too quickly. A problem teenagers (that's you) have when it comes to growing up is playing what I'll call the grownup game. It's the 'game' of wanting to be treated as an adult when it is convenient to your advantage but then reverting to being a kid when *that's* to your advantage. EXAMPLE: Leesa relentlessly begged her parents to let her drive to a major city with her best friend to attend a concert. Leesa, who had just turned eighteen, had never driven in a big city and had never been in a heavy traffic environment. But she finally wore them down with comments about being eighteen, that she would be going to college in a few months, and that she had to learn to do things independently at some point.

The trip went reasonably smooth—only two wrong turns, but neither was a big deal. The 'big deal'...the big deal happened when Leesa and her friend came out of the concert. Her car was gone! Leesa and her friend first thought the car had been stolen, but it only took a minute for Leesa's friend to see the NO PARKING...NO EXCEPTIONS...ALL CARS WILL BE TOWED sign. The two girls hadn't been paying close enough attention. They were too busy checking their hair and make-up, calling Leesa's parents to tell them they had made the trip without any problems, and congratulating themselves on finding free parking instead of paying $25 to park in the garage.

Leesa called the number on the sign, gave them a sob story about this being her first time driving the car this far and not seeing the warning sign, and asked what she had to do to get her car. They were not impressed by her story and told her she could get her car as soon as she paid the $300 fee. She called Uber for a ride, then called her dad to tell him she would need his credit card for the fee.

Guess what? He said no. Well, sort of. He said he would pay the fee over the phone with his card but then transfer the money from her savings account into his. She was not happy. It wasn't her fault, she said. She couldn't help it that she didn't see the sign. She needed that money for other stuff—namely, prom. Guess what? Her dad said that was too bad.

Leesa wanted to be treated as an adult until she didn't want to be.

Guess what? You cannot have it both ways. You cannot pick and choose when you want to be an adult and when you don't want to be. That doesn't mean you should be thrown into the pool's deep end from the get-go. It would be best if you could grow up a little at a time. You also need to prove you can handle the responsibilities of being grown-up and enjoying its privileges. Take ownership of your actions without excuses when mistakes happen. That is a part of embracing yourself as a human being and a sign of growing up.

Reality Check

Have you ever felt like Leesa—like you should be given the privileges of being treated like an adult without having to live up to its responsibilities? I know the answer. It's yes. I know it's yes because everyone does. It's part of the growing-up process. Or maybe I should say that discovering that you must learn to enjoy and deal with *both* is the growing-up process.

The same thing is true when it comes to your relationship with Jesus. Jesus did not expect the disciples to be qualified and ready for ministry right from the start. He told them to drop all their worldly possessions and follow him so he could *make them into* fishers for men. Then, after he had assembled his team, he poured himself into them through teaching, deep conversations, setting an example, working with them, laughing with them, developing deep friendships with them, praying with and for them, mentoring them, holding them accountable, loving them and their families, preparing them for the future, and just doing life with them in general.

If you read through the Gospels, you will see that Jesus kept his disciples close to him for a while, then eventually sent them out in pairs of two to teach, preach, and heal. Then, after he had been resurrected and returned to heaven, the disciples, for the most part, went out on their own. They had grown and matured to be ready to go out on their own. But even then, they didn't stay alone. Some of them met up throughout the years. Some went into ministry with other faithful Christians. And others, from what little we know, went on to be effective evangelists worldwide, working independently to spread the message of salvation.

No matter which route they took, it is evident that they were mature enough and grown-up enough in their love, knowledge, wisdom, and commitment to God and Christianity to handle it. Why? Because they went through the process.

The process of making tough decisions or transitioning into living on your own. Another example would be handling the freedom of college and, most importantly, making your faith your own by being part of the Church vs. doing church. All these things are part of the growing-up process. Growing up is something we all must do. It is something almost everyone wants to do. The key to doing it gracefully is to do it in phases and stages and to be ready to accept and deal with each phase's share of good, bad, and between.

Mirror, Mirror...

Let's take a long, hard look at this.

1: How often do you expect to be treated as an adult until you don't want to be? What are some things you have said or done to indicate this?

2: What about your spiritual life? What are you doing to become a more mature Christian?

Take a few minutes to read the following verses. What do they say to you personally about the current season of life that you are in?

- *Hear, my son, your father's instruction, and forsake not your mother's teaching, for they are a graceful garland for your head and pendants for your neck. ~Proverbs 1:8-9 (ESV)*
- *Children, obey your parents in the Lord, for this is right. "Honor your father and mother"—which is the first commandment with a promise—"so that it may go well*

with you and that you may enjoy long life on the earth."
~Ephesians 6:1-3 (NIV)

- *Even small children are known by their actions, so is their conduct really pure and upright? ~Proverbs 20:11 (NIV)*
- *So flee youthful passions and pursue righteousness, faith, love, and peace, along with those who call on the Lord from a pure heart. ~2nd Timothy 2:22 (ESV)*

Pray

Are you praying to be more mature in your faith? Are you praying to be more mature in your decision-making or the way you treat other people? Ask God to give you wisdom, the ability to think before you speak or act, a selfless attitude, and to take the time to measure everything you see and do according to God's Word, which is the infallible truth.

25

THERE'S NOTHING FREAKY ABOUT SHARING JESUS WITH OTHER PEOPLE

And I heard the voice of the Lord saying, "Whom shall I send, and who will go for us?" Then I said, "Here am I! Send me."

— *ISAIAH 6:8 (ESV)*

S end me? Where? And to do what?

Yes, you. When you accept Jesus as your Lord and Savior, it is a promise to God to use your gift of salvation for your benefit, the benefit of others, and to do both in ways that honor and praise God.

Where? Wherever you are on any given day. At home. At school. At work. On the field. In a club meeting. At the gym. At the mall. When you are hanging out with your friends—guys and girls.

What...or how? There are a million things you can do. Most of them happen without thinking about it—once you get into the habit.

I know you have temptations coming at you from all angles. Some of them...a lot of them, even, are things you don't even realize are temptations. You might think these things are just part of everyday life as a teenage girl. I'm talking about gossiping, complaining, lying to your parents, and shunning someone because of their clothes or the street they live on. Things like foul language, drinking, drugs, and making out or having sex. Just because they are expected from the world's perspective doesn't make them good. Just because something is legal doesn't make it spiritual. Even if those things are not on your to-do list for the weekend doesn't make them any less wrong. And that's where you come in. God is sending YOU to make a difference...to be the difference in the world around you, even if that world is no bigger than a few friends and your family.

Reality Check

Fact: Jesus' last words before returning to heaven are known as The Great Commission. You can read them in Matthew 28:19-20. The first two words he says in these verses are, "**So** go...." Not "Hey, if you have time...." Or "It might be nice if you would...." Or "God and I would appreciate it if you would....". Jesus' 'So go....' isn't a suggestion or a request. It is a command. Jesus expects us to tell others who he is and what he has done for us because we don't want to keep it to ourselves. Because we want other people to have what we have, which is forgiveness, an eternity in heaven, and the blessings that come with God's unconditional love.

Fact: In Mathew chapter five, Jesus told us to let our light shine. He also said that people would know we belong to him by our words and actions—loving other people as he does. James wrote that faith without works is dead (James 2:20). So, it's not a matter of if. It's a matter of how and when, and where.

Remember a few paragraphs ago when I said there are a million things you can do? Well, it's time to list a few of them to motivate you.

- Post a Bible verse on your social media once a week. Start a conversation on how that verse speaks to you.
- Wear your church's t-shirt or t-shirt with a scripture on it. You'll never know when you might come across someone looking for a home church.
- Be active in your school's FCA (Fellowship of Christian Athletes) club.
- Try to choose church over any other activity. Don't miss church for a soccer game or slumber party at a

friend's house. Don't skip out on youth groups or a service project because you want to hang out with your friends. Take your friends with you—or at least invite them to go along.

- Don't get caught up in gossip, complaining, mean girl drama, guy/girl drama, or cliques. These actions will keep you feeling low and disconnected from your Spirit.
- Don't talk to or about teachers, your parents, coaches, or peers disrespectfully.
- Don't just say no to things you shouldn't do and sit at home feeling sorry for yourself. Do what a friend of mine calls the 'Your Terms…Your Turf's way of having fun. Take a friend with you on a walk and talk. You could host game nights, picnics, movie nights, spa parties, or whatever else makes you smile for yourself and your friends. This way, you are in control of what is and isn't allowed. And trust me— everyone will have a great time.
- Make sure the clothes you wear, the movies you watch, the places you go, and the words you speak reflect whom you are supposed to be—a child of the One True God.

See? It's not about being sent to some third-world country or working in full-time ministry. Being sent is about being the hands and feet of Jesus no matter where you are, who you are with, or what you are doing. Being sent is about having a heart and mind that think and act the way Jesus did when he was here on earth. The more you adopt the "Being Sent" mindset, the more it becomes a part of you. He does not expect you to be perfect or start preaching in the streets. You can still wear a pretty, sparkly dress to prom or spend lazy afternoons at the pool with your friends talking about the latest fashions and hairstyles. Jesus does not expect you to be perfect, feel like you must constantly walk on eggshells, or not have any fun in life. Enjoy your life! You are honoring God, Jesus, and yourself by living up to your full potential, being genuinely kind to others, and having a "Being Sent" mindset.

Is it hard? Sometimes. Is it scary? Sometimes. Will it cost you a few friends and invitations? Yes. But the 'friends' you lose and the invitations you don't get aren't the ones you need in your life, anyway. And here's something else you need to know. You will never be alone. The Spirit living *in* you, the Spirit of God himself, is always there, ready, willing, and able to give you the words to say, the confidence and courage you need, and protect your heart from unkind words or actions. You have to invite Him in and let Him. Let the Holy Spirit deal with these things instead of trying to do it alone.

Being sent by God isn't like your mom sending you to the store for bread and cereal. Being sent by God is a way of life. It's up to you, though, whether it's YOUR way of life.

Mirror, Mirror...

How many of your friends know you are a Christian?

Are you giving them an accurate representation of what it means to be a Christian?

Do you see yourself striving to be a better person than you were yesterday?

Do you lead by example and let your words' kindness, actions' thoughtfulness, and unconditional love for others speak for themselves?

How comfortable would you be if Jesus in the flesh was your sidekick for the next week and you didn't alter your schedule or activities in any way?

When was the last time you decided what to do based on what Jesus would do vs. what someone else expected or wanted you to do?

Just a few things to think about...and pray about.

Pray

Each time you pray, ask Jesus to give you the courage and confidence to be like him no matter what. Ask him to bless you for being faithful to him by giving you friends who respect and appreciate your faith and commitment to God.

26

WHY DO PEOPLE THINK THAT CHURCH IS IMPORTANT?

And let us consider how we may spur one another on toward love and good deeds, not giving up meeting together, as some are in the habit of doing, but encouraging one another—and all the more as you see the Day approaching.

— *HEBREWS 10:24-25 (NIV)*

F or *almost* as long as the Church has been in existence (the Day of Pentecost in Acts 2 tells you all about it), people have been trying to come up with their way of doing church instead of doing it according to God's way. Instead of being a part of a church community, some say they can only get close to God in the woods, along the banks of a river or shores of a lake, or even from the comfort of their home in front of the television or laptop. The people who say they are better off not going to a church because it's full of hypocrites, so what's the point? And now you have a group of people who refuse to go to church who are riddled with fear and anxiety to even leave their own homes because of the events that have taken place in recent years. What all these groups of people have in common is that they are alone. Don't get me wrong; I love a good prayer and meditation session in the woods. Even Jesus knew when to recharge and have alone time with God in nature (Luke 5:16). If Jesus needed to do that, then we should too, Amen. Let us pray for anyone alone, lost, and feeling spiritually blocked off that they find their way back to their loving church community.

Okay, so yes, there are times when you should stay home— like when you are sick or recovering from surgery or an injury. There are also those whose immune system is compromised to the point that it would be dangerous— someone on chemo, for example. And yes, some people cannot go due to mobility issues, age-related health problems (like dementia), or maybe someone is a caretaker of very young babies or the elderly. God gets that. He understands.

But hear me loud and clear when I say that sleeping in, studying for a test, finishing homework you've had the entire weekend to work on, hanging with your friends, going someplace fun, or the attitude of 'I don't feel like going,' 'church is boring,' 'there's nothing for me there,' 'I don't get anything out of it,' or any of the other 1001 excuses people give, are not valid reasons for not going to church. Nope... not that one either (the one you are thinking in your head right now). And here's why none of those things work as a hall pass: the Bible says otherwise.

Do not give up meeting together. We have learned in recent years just how vital it is for human connection and doing whatever it takes to keep yourself surrounded by a loving and supportive community. Exodus 20, where we read the Ten Commandments God gave Moses, starts with this; "You shall have no other gods before me.". Nothing is supposed to come between God and us. So, since God says to come together to worship him…. In 1st Corinthians, God inspired Paul to write about serving, worshiping, and working *together* as a family and body of believers. We cannot help or encourage one another, learn with and from each other, or worship with each other when we are not together. Romans 1:12 says we must mutually inspire each other. Throughout the book of Acts, we read about Christians coming together daily, even to worship, encourage, listen, and learn about the teaching of Jesus.

Are you beginning to see a pattern here? I sure hope so. Don't do life alone.

Reality Check

How well would you do in trig if you didn't pay attention in class and do the work? Or what chair would you be sitting in the band if you never practiced? How much time do you think you would spend sitting on the bench if you only bothered to show up for practice when you didn't have anything better to do? You didn't even have to think about the answers to those questions, did you? They were immediate and automatic, weren't they?

Hello! Your relationship with God and your level of growth and maturity as a Christian depend on attending, participating, and serving in your church. Oh, and one more thing—your relationship with God is more important than sports, band, and trig.

In reality, church attendance AND active participation in your church are not an option as far as God is concerned. You NEED to be there. You NEED to be an active part of what's happening there. Why?

- Because you cannot learn how to use, study, and understand the Bible on your own. FYI: the trees don't talk, and you can't ask questions to the people on TV or Youtube.
- Because we are expected to help other Christians and let them help us.
- Because we are expected to fellowship with other Christians, Fellowship (hanging out, having fun,

eating with them...) with other Christians is a safety net of sorts. It makes us stronger as Christians (there is strength in numbers). It helps cut down on the temptations to do things we shouldn't. It builds deeper friendships with people who won't try to pull us away from God. It lets us encourage other people and be a true friends to them. It gives us opportunities to use our God-given talents and abilities in ways that put a smile on God's face. It's an incredible feeling to know you have a community of people you can count on and who depend on you.

- Because the Bible commands us to come together to take communion, pray for each other, sing praises, and worship God together as a family.
- Because it is God's plan for His people.

Another reality that needs to be covered is this: being part of the Church and your local church isn't supposed to be about what you get out of it. The purpose is to give back to God. Give him praise, honor, and yourself (talent, time, attention). He turns around and gives you even more blessings when you do those things. You grant to Him; He gives more to you. You give more to Him. He provides even more to you. In other words, God's way of saying thanks for putting Him first is to bless you.

Mirror, Mirror...

How faithful are you in attending *and* participating in your church? Remember, keeping a seat warm and participating actively in the church are two different things. There are so many ways to volunteer at church. I am on the host committee. My job is to help people feel welcomed and seen as they come in. I clean up from the previous service, set up the chairs for communion or with flyers, and welcome people with a huge smile as they walk in for the next service. It is so rewarding! I know it's a huge help, and it costs me nothing. I've met amazing people doing it and feel planted in my church. It's a win-win.

What are the reasons for the answers to the previous question?

If your answers are like, 'my parents make me,' 'it's a habit,' 'I don't mind going, but I don't get anything out of it,' then quite honestly, you've got work to do. It's also no wonder you are struggling. Your relationship with the Church and your home church needs to become *personal* and *sincere.*

If you are already genuinely looking for God and trying to take your relationship with Him to the next level(s), keep going. You are on the right track. When you look for God with your whole heart, you will find Him. He is not hiding. He is merely waiting for you to come to Him. Why is He waiting? Because despite His power, He is not pushy.

Pray

Ask God to open your heart so that you genuinely love going to church to worship, praise, learn, and fellowship with other Christians. Ask God to open your mind and your eyes to what He wants you to do in your church so that you will feel more a part of it. Ask God to give you closer relationships with other Christian teenagers so that you will know you are not alone in your school and your community.

27

HOW DO I KNOW FOR SURE?

Faith is confidence in what we hope for and assurance about what we do not see.

— *HEBREWS 11:1 (NIV)*

I f you have been to church, this verse on faith is one you have probably heard several times. A whole lot. There's a reason for that. It's because faith is what brings us to God. It is what we HAVE TO HAVE to be able to accept Jesus' gift of salvation.

We cannot see God, Jesus, or the Holy Spirit. But we can see evidence of their existence and power. We can see and hear how they work in our lives and the lives of others. We can see and hear God's Word, which is God's voice and testimonies of those who did see and experience Jesus in the flesh. But even those people and even people like Moses who spoke to God and Daniel who experienced some incredible miracles from God were operating on faith.

Think about it—Daniel's faith and devotion to God kept him praying even when he was told not to. And it was because of his faith that God was faith*ful* to Daniel by protecting him from the lions. Abraham, Noah, Shadrach, Meshach, Abednego, Elijah, David, Hannah, Moses, Moses' mom...on and on the list goes of people in the Old Testament who had faith.

You also need to remember that the faith these people had didn't come after God did something to daze and amaze them. God didn't tell Hannah she would have a baby if she promised to give the baby to full-time ministry. She gave Samuel back to God because he answered her prayer. Noah didn't build the ark after God gave him a play-by-play of what would happen. He made it because God said so. Abraham's faith in God's promise to create an entire people group from him and his descendants gave Abraham the level of trust he needed to take Isaac up the mountain with him. He *knew because of faith* that God would provide another sacrifice.

But it didn't end there. People who followed Jesus watched him, listened to him, and even received a miracle from him didn't see 'how' Jesus did these things. They believed he could, though, because of faith. One of the most beautiful examples of this in the entire Bible is found in John, chapter nine.

In this account, the Pharisees, who were always out to trip Jesus up, questioned a man who had been born blind but was now miraculously able to see…thanks to Jesus. The Pharisees relentlessly hounded this man (and his parents), trying to get him to incriminate Jesus as a sinner and lawbreaker because this all took place on the Sabbath (when no work was to be done).

The man got tired of the questioning and finally said (paraphrased), "I don't know if he's a sinner or not. But here is one thing I know—I was blind, but now I can see."

The man didn't know much about Jesus, but he knew enough to trust (have faith) that whatever Jesus told him to do had meaning and purpose. In this case, it was for Jesus to give the man his sight and for the man to give Jesus his heart.

Faith is being fully convinced that something is genuine and authentic vs. contemplating whether it is or not.

Reality Check

You have faith in many things. You have confidence that there will be clean knives in the drawer when you want to make a PBJ. You have faith that your toothpaste will not suddenly taste like onions. You have faith that it will go through when you reply to a text. You have confidence that your parents will not move while you are at school and will not tell you. You probably don't even think about those things as faith, do you? You assume everything will be how it's supposed to be because it always is. Well, guess what? That's faith. It's the same *kind* of faith that **can and should** tell you that God and Jesus will always come through and that the promises they've made will always be kept because they have an everlasting love for you, are forever faithful, and have never *broken* promises. Question: When you think of it in those terms, does it make it any easier to wrap your head around?

Nikki was raised not to believe in God. She thought she had to have proof of everything before it could be viewed as truth. So, when she came to church camp with a friend, she did not waste any time telling one of the teachers she didn't believe in God for several reasons, but the main reason was that no one could prove He existed. She said, "I don't believe anything I cannot prove."

The teacher asked how she went about proving everything. "How do you prove what you read in school? What do you hear or read on the news?" Nikki replied that those sources had researched and proven their facts, making them believable.

"But how do you *know* they did their research? Aren't you trusting or having faith in them that they did? And what about false information? What if someone reported that potatoes didn't grow in the ground—that it was all a hoax and then went on to present 'facts' to prove their theory? Would you consider that true?"

Nikki laughed and said that would be easy to disprove because of the proof that already existed that says potatoes grow in the ground. "Exactly!" the teacher said. "The same is true about God. There is way more proof of His existence than anyone can disprove. No one has been able to disprove God. So...."

Nikki admitted the teacher had a point. She still didn't believe in God, but she realized her thought process wasn't as foolproof as she'd thought. Nikki, for all her doubts and denials about faith, had it. She was just putting it in the wrong people, places, and things. What about you?

Mirror, Mirror...

How would you describe your faith in God? How does it compare to your faith in other people and things?

What makes you doubt God? What makes you doubt His faithfulness to you?

These are questions you need to ask yourself. You also need to find the answers and do the things God says will help our faith grow. Pray. Read the Bible. Ask God to take care of problems and situations instead of trying to handle everything on your own. Don't just ask. Listen and watch for His answers and follow through on doing things His way.

Take some time this week and in the future to read the following accounts of people who had faith in God and Jesus. Use these examples to help you grow your faith.

- 1st Kings 17 (Elijah)
- Joshua chapters 5 and 10 (Joshua)
- Malachi 3:10
- Acts 9:1-19 (Ananias)
- Acts 9:32-43 (Dorcas)
- Mark 5:21-43 (Jesus' miracles)

Pray

Ask God for faith. Ask God to give you opportunities to grow your faith…and then take them.

THE WAY, TRUTH, AND LIFE

Jesus answered, "I am the way and the truth and the life. No one comes to the Father except through me.

— *JOHN 14:6 (NIV)*

The verse above is much like the one on faith from the last chapter. It is one you have heard repeatedly. It seems straightforward, doesn't it? Jesus says that he is the way and that anyone who wants to be with the Father must go through Jesus. There's not much room for debate—or at least you wouldn't think so. But over the centuries, it has become quite an issue. That is why so many different denominations (different kinds of churches) exist. It is not anyone's place to judge another for what denomination their heart and life path have led them down. It's like saying your way of connecting to God and loving Jesus is better than someone else's. That's not what Christianity is all about or what Jesus wanted for his people.

Discussions and debates about why so many different denominations have been going on for centuries are still ongoing today. To compare them against each other would be a massive undertaking without any end and is not the purpose of this book. So, I'm not going to do that. Besides, there is no reason to, because no matter what anyone else says, thinks, or believes, Jesus' opinion on the subject is the only one that counts. It is the only truth, which is why that is the only thing we will look at in this last 'official' chapter.

This is important stuff. Your salvation and where you spend eternity depend on your acceptance of these truths and your willingness to make them YOUR truths and YOUR life's purpose. Are you? Or, at the very least, are you willing to consider it? To at least try?

Your salvation is found in only Jesus. Your faith is to be in Jesus. Your hope for eternity in heaven is because of Jesus, so it only makes sense to look at what God the Father and Jesus the Son say about how we come to the Father through Jesus. That is why I want you to take some time to read through each of these verses a couple of times; stopping to let the words wash over you and seep into your brain and your heart. Own these words. Own your relationship with God. Own your faith. Claim your salvation.

Matthew 3:13-17 (NIV): Then Jesus came from Galilee to the Jordan to be baptized by John. But John tried to deter him, saying, "I need to be baptized by you, and do you come to me?" Jesus replied, "Let it be so now; it is proper for us to do this to fulfill all righteousness." Then John consented. As soon as Jesus was baptized, he went up out of the water. At that moment, heaven was opened, and he saw the Spirit of God descending like a dove and alighting on him. And a voice from heaven said, "This is my Son, whom I love; with him, I am well pleased." Even though Jesus was sinless, he was baptized by immersion to fulfill righteousness. That's Bible language for 'submitting to God' or 'conforming to God's expectations. That should say to you: If it pleases God, which it did, then that should be reason enough to obey. Plus, if it was good enough for Jesus to be baptized, it should be good enough for us.

Luke 6:40 (NIV): A disciple is not above his teacher, but everyone, when fully trained, will be like his teacher. This verse syncs with what you just read about following in Jesus' footsteps and that no one is better or "above" anybody else. Psalm 199:105 (ESV): Your word is a lamp to my feet and a light to my path. God's Word is the final authority on all things and will guide you throughout life.

Acts 2:36-38 (NIV): Therefore, let all Israel be assured of this: God has made this Jesus, whom you crucified, both

Lord and Messiah. When the people heard this, they were cut to the heart and said to Peter and the other apostles, "Brothers, what shall we do?" Peter replied, "Repent and be baptized, every one of you, in the name of Jesus Christ for the forgiveness of your sins. And you will receive the gift of the Holy Spirit. Do you notice the progression here? The people heard. Then they believed what they heard and confessed their sins because they wanted to be saved by Jesus. For that to happen, they had to repent, a complete 360 on how they believed and lived, and be baptized to wash their sins away symbolically. At that point, the Holy Spirit took up residence in each individual to give spiritual guidance, strength, wisdom, and comfort.

John 3:1-5 (NIV): Now, there was a Pharisee named Nicodemus, a member of the Jewish ruling council. He came to Jesus at night and said, "Rabbi, we know that you are a teacher who has come from God. No one could perform the signs you are doing if God were not with him." Jesus replied, "Truly I tell you, no one can see the kingdom of God unless they are born again. "How can someone be born when they are old?" Nicodemus asked. "Surely, they cannot enter a second time into their mother's womb to be born!" Jesus answered, "Very truly I tell you, no one can enter the kingdom of God unless they are born of water and the Spirit. Jesus is crystal-clear on this. Unless a person is born again— comes out of the water—as a baby comes out of the amniotic water of its mom, they cannot be 'born' into God's family.

Mark 16:16 (ESV): Whoever believes and is baptized will be saved, but whoever does not believe will be condemned. Acts 22:16 (ESV): And now why do you wait? Rise and be baptized and wash away your sins, calling on his name.

1Peter 3:10 (ESV): Baptism, which corresponds to *this*, now saves you, not as a removal of dirt from the body but as an appeal to God for a good conscience, through the resurrection of Jesus Christ. The 'this' he is referring to is the flood—the one God used to destroy the earth and everyone alive (except Noah and his family) so that he could start over. This is another example of how God used water to wash creation clean, so to speak, just like we are made clean and new when we are baptized. It's a fresh start.

John 3:16 (NIV): For God so loved the world that he gave his one and only Son, that whoever believes in him shall not perish but have eternal life. This is one more of those famous verses that nearly everyone knows. The glitch is in some people's perception or interpretation of the word 'believes.' They think the word means to accept something as truth and be confident in that knowledge—the 'something' is that Jesus is God's son and that he died for our sins. Don't get me wrong—that is hugely important. It's the first step, remember? But the Greek word used in this verse is the word 'Pistis' (don't laugh). It means to entrust, i.e., hand over, fully obey, and be forever faithful. That's a bit more involved than admitting Jesus paid the price for your sin and rose again, isn't it?

As you can see, there is so much emphasis on being baptized and born again throughout the New Testament. If you have never been baptized, or maybe, you were as a baby and want to do it again as an outward expression of what has shifted in your heart, you can do that!

The Bible has the rest of the story, so to speak, and is where you need to go for all things related to God. The purpose of this book has been to guide you toward the Bible by sorting through issues that I know from experience are on the hearts and minds of every teenage girl searching for the truth about God and trying to figure out how to have the best possible relationship with Him. My prayer is that I have been able to help you discover ways to make your relationship with God personal to you. This is paramount for your journey in life and will affect how you conquer life's obstacles, interact with people, and embrace yourself. Do not see your struggles as failures. See your struggles for what they are—opportunities for growth and admitting that you cannot do life alone. You need God to come alongside you and fight. And when you let God fight with you...when you put him out in front, you can't lose. Do you get that? YOU CAN NOT LOSE!

LETTER FROM THE AUTHOR

Dear Beloved Reader,

I pray that having made it to the end of the book, you now have a greater sense of confidence and are ready to accomplish the life you are meant to live. More importantly, I pray that you feel a deeper connection with God. I hope this book has helped you realize how loved you are—by your people, our Heavenly Father, and me.

Do not keep this love to yourself. Please share it! You have the love that will make a massive impact in this world. Random acts of kindness are something we Christians should get into the habit of doing. They are a form of service and generosity. And do not forget that when we bless others, God turns around and blesses us tenfold!

One thing you can do to be a blessing to your peers is to encourage other girls to read this book. There are girls out there who feel alone, unloved or lost. You may have someone in mind right now. There are also girls out there who know whom Jesus is and have accepted him as Savior but may not have encountered him on a personal level. So, if this book has impacted you in any way, I hope you will tell other girls about the book by taking a couple of minutes to leave an honest review on Amazon. Seriously, it only takes two minutes. If you could impact another girl's life by giving up two minutes of your time, would you? By leaving a review, you are doing precisely what Jesus told us to do: ' go' and spread the message. Pretty cool, huh? Let's spread the word of God and make an impact on young women together.

Scan the QR code below to leave a quick review!

Thank you from the bottom of my heart. May God continue to bless you beyond your wildest dreams and help you reach your fullest potential.

Love,

Hillary Olive

Ephesians 3: 14-19

SPECIAL GIFT JUST FOR YOU!

THIS BUNDLE INCLUDES:

A 'CONNECT WITH CHRIST' WORKSHEET TO HELP YOU DETERMINE WHAT IS HOLDING YOU BACK FROM HAVING THE CONNECTION YOU NEED

'FEELING SOME TYPE OF WAY' LIST OF 15 SCRIPTURES YOU CAN JUMP TO AT ANY TIME WHEN LIFE GETS HARD

'HOST, LEAD, AND SUCCEED' YOUR STEP-BY-STEP GUIDE TO CREATING A BRAND NEW BIBLE STUDY GROUP

CITATIONS PAGE

Borenstein, J. Dr. (2020, July 9). *Self-love and what it means* Brain & Behavior Research Foundation. Retrieved June 15, 2022, from https://www. bbrfoundation.org/blog/self-love-and-what-it-means

Burnett, N. W. (2007). *Calm in the face of the storm: Spiritual daily practice for the peacemaker*. Devenio Restituo Pacis Publishers.

Lipka, M. (2020, May 30). Five *facts about prayer*. Pew Research Center. Retrieved June 16, 2022, from https://www.pewresearch.org/fact-tank/ 2016/05/04/5-facts-about-prayer/